NOTES FROM UNDERGROUND

Fyodor Dostoevsky

EDITORIAL DIRECTOR Justin Kestler
EXECUTIVE EDITOR Ben Florman

SERIES EDITORS Boomie Aglietti, John Crowther, Justin Kestler
PRODUCTION Christian Lorentzen

WRITER Caolan Madden
EDITORS Matt Blanchard, John Crowther

This edition published by Spark Publishing

Spark Publishing
A Division of SparkNotes LLC
120 Fifth Avenue, 8th Floor
New York, NY 10011

02 03 04 05 SN 9 8 7 6 5 4 3 2 1

Please send all comments and questions or report errors to feedback@sparknotes.com.

Library of Congress information available upon request

Printed and bound in the United States

RRD-C

ISBN 1-58663-817-3

INTRODUCTION: STOPPING TO BUY SPARKNOTES ON A SNOWY EVENING

Whose words these are you *think* you know.
Your paper's due tomorrow, though;
We're glad to see you stopping here
To get some help before you go.

Lost your course? You'll find it here.
Face tests and essays without fear.
Between the words, good grades at stake:
Get great results throughout the year.

Once school bells caused your heart to quake
As teachers circled each mistake.
Use SparkNotes and no longer weep,
Ace every single test you take.

Yes, books are lovely, dark, and deep,
But only what you grasp you keep,
With hours to go before you sleep,
With hours to go before you sleep.

Contents

Context

FYODOR DOSTOEVSKY IS RENOWNED AS one of the world's greatest novelists and literary psychologists. Born in Moscow in 1821, the son of a doctor, Dostoevsky was educated first at home and then at a boarding school. When he was a young boy, his father sent him to the St. Petersburg Academy of Military Engineering, from which he graduated in 1843. Dostoevsky had long been interested in writing, and after graduation he immediately resigned from his minor military post to devote his time to his craft. His first novel, *Poor Folk* (1846), was immediately popular with critics.

Dostoevsky's early view of the world was shaped by his experiences with social injustice. At the age of twenty-six, Dostoevsky became active in socialist circles, largely because of his opposition to the institution of serfdom. His political opinions were influenced by his experiences as a young boy—his father was murdered by his own serfs while Dostoevsky was away at school. Another experience that greatly affected Dostevsky, and that found its way into his writing, was the time he spent in prison. In April 1849, Dostoevsky was arrested for his participation in a group that illegally printed and distributed socialist propaganda. After spending eight months in prison, Dostoevsky was sentenced to death and was led, with other members of the group, to be shot. But the execution turned out to be only a show, meant to punish the prisoners psychologically. After his brush with death, Dostoevsky spent four years at a Siberian labor camp and then served in the military for another four years. During his time in prison, he rejected his extreme socialist views in favor of an adherence to traditional, conservative Russian values—a change in ideology that is evident throughout his later works.

Dostoevsky spent most of the 1860s in western Europe, immersing himself in the European culture that he believed was encroaching on Russia—an issue he explores in *Notes from Underground*. These years in Europe were a difficult time for Dostoevsky, as he struggled with poverty, epilepsy, and an addiction to gambling. The publication of *Crime and Punishment* (1866), however, brought him a reversal of fortune, earning him popular and critical success and rescuing him from financial disaster. His later novel *The Brothers Karamazov* (1880) brought him further critical success.

Dostoevsky was one of the pioneers of realism in the modern novel, and *Notes from Underground* (1864), along with his later novels, belongs to this genre. Realist writers—Honoré de Balzac in France, Charles Dickens in England, and Nikolai Gogol and Dostoevsky in Russia, among others—reexamined the entire purpose of the novel. Realism focused on "real" people, generally city dwellers, prostitutes, poor students, lowly craftsmen, and other types of characters who had been merely subjects of ridicule or providers of comic relief in previous literature. Prior to realism, everyday life had been considered below literature, which was meant to rise above the mundane. Dostoevsky's work, often seen as the culmination of realism, aims not to rise above reality, but to portray it in all its complexity and difficulty.

Notes from Underground played an important role in the development of realist fiction. The novel probes the mind of an individual on the margins of modern society, and examines the effects modern life has on that man's personality. The protagonist is a low-ranking civil servant in 1860s St. Petersburg who has gradually gone mad over a lifetime of inability to cope with the society around him. The Underground Man is an antihero, the kind of downtrodden, indecisive victim of society that Dostoevsky would continue to explore in his later works.

Dostoevsky may have been prompted to write *Notes from Underground* in response to a revolutionary novel called *What Is to Be Done?* (1863), written by the "rational egoist" N. G. Chernyshevsky. Rational egoism held that life could be perfected solely through the application of reason and enlightened self-interest. Along with many other radical social thinkers of the 1860s, the rational egoists put great emphasis on the powers of reason and natural law—principles ostensibly derived from inherent properties of the world. The rational egoists' theories grew out of the social liberalism of the 1840s, in which Dostoevsky was interested.

During his prison time in Siberia, however, Dostoevsky learned that the peasants and undereducated workers of Russia associated progressive thinkers with the upper classes that oppressed them and limited their freedom. He decided that the theorists of the 1860s were too absorbed in European culture, and too far removed from inherently Russian values. Dostoevsky grew to believe that the way to create harmony among all Russian people was through a return to traditional Russian values, such as personal responsibility, religion, brotherly love, and the family. He believed that theories that seek universal social laws to explain and govern human behavior ignore the fundamental individuality of the human soul, the complexity of human personality, and the power of free will.

The Underground Man in *Notes from Underground* is both a mouthpiece for Dostoevsky's ideas and an example of the kind of problems that modern Russian society inevitably produced. Like Dostoevsky, the Underground Man is critical of rational egoism and other dangerously totalitarian visions of utopia. He is extremely critical of dogmatism of any kind. At the same time, he is a victim of the modern Russian urban experience. Deprived of positive social interactions, the Underground Man tries to relate to the world according to the codes and examples he finds in European literature. The failure of these attempts makes him even more bitter and isolated, driving him deeper underground.

Plot Overview

THE ANONYMOUS NARRATOR of *Notes from Underground* is a bitter, misanthropic man living alone in St. Petersburg, Russia, in the 1860s. He is a veteran of the Russian civil service who has recently been able to retire because he has inherited some money. The novel consists of the "notes" that the man writes, a confused and often contradictory set of memoirs or confessions describing and explaining his alienation from modern society.

Notes from Underground is divided into two sections. The first, "Underground," is shorter and set in the 1860s, when the Underground Man is forty years old. This section serves as an introduction to the character of the Underground Man, explaining his theories about his antagonistic position toward society.

The first words we hear from the Underground Man tell us that he is "a sick man . . . a wicked man . . . an unattractive man" whose self-loathing and spite has crippled and corrupted him. He is a well-read and highly intelligent man, and he believes that this fact accounts for his misery. The Underground Man explains that, in modern society, all conscious and educated men should be as miserable as he is. He has become disillusioned with all philosophy. He has appreciation for the sublime, Romantic idea of "the beautiful and lofty," but he is aware of its absurdity in the context of his narrow, mundane existence.

The Underground Man has great contempt for nineteenth-century utilitarianism, a school of thought that attempted to use mathematical formulas and logical proofs to align man's desires with his best interests. The Underground Man complains that man's primary desire is to exercise his free will, whether or not it is in his best interests. In the face of utilitarianism, man will do nasty and unproductive things simply to prove that his free will is unpredictable and therefore completely free. This assertion partially explains the Underground Man's insistence that he takes pleasure in his own toothaches or liver pains: such pleasure in pain is a way of spiting the comfortable predictability of life in modern society, which accepts without question the value of going to the doctor. The Underground Man is not proud of all this useless behavior, however. He has enormous contempt for himself as a human being. He is aware that he is so overcome by inertia that he cannot even become wicked enough to be a scoundrel, or insignificant enough to be an insect, or lazy enough to be a true lazybones.

The second fragment of *Notes from Underground,* entitled "Apropos of the Wet Snow," describes specific events in the Underground Man's life in the 1840s, when he was twenty-four years old. In a sense, this section serves as a practical illustration of the more abstract ideas the Underground Man sets forth in the first section. This second section reveals the narrator's progression from his youthful perspective, influenced by Romanticism and ideals of "the beautiful and lofty," to his mature perspective in 1860, which is purely cynical about beauty, loftiness, and literariness in general.

"Apropos of the Wet Snow" describes interactions between the Underground Man and various people who inhabit his world: soldiers, former schoolmates, and prostitutes. The Underground Man is so alienated from these people that he is completely incapable of normal interaction with them. He treats them with a mixture of disgust and fear that results in his own effacement or humiliation—which in turn result in remorse and self-loathing.

The Underground Man's alienation manifests itself in all kinds of relationships. When walking in the park, he obsesses about whether to yield the right of way to a soldier whom he does not even know. Then, in a confused attempt at social interaction, the Underground Man deliberately follows some school acquaintances to a dinner where he is not wanted, alternately insulting them openly and craving their attention and friendship. Later that same evening, the Underground Man attempts to rescue an attractive young prostitute named Liza by delivering impassioned, sentimental speeches about the terrible fate that awaits her if she continues to sell her body.

When Liza comes to visit the Underground Man in his shoddy apartment several days later, he reacts with shame and anger when he realizes she has reason to pity or look down upon him. The Underground Man continues to insult Liza throughout the visit. Hurt and confused, she leaves him alone in his apartment.

Here the Underground Man decides to end his notes. In a footnote at the end of the novel, Dostoevsky reveals that the Underground Man fails to make even this simple decision to stop writing, as Dostoevsky says that the manuscript of the notes goes on for many pages beyond the point at which he has chosen to cut it off.

Character List

The Underground Man The anonymous narrator and protagonist of the novel. The Underground Man is a minor civil servant living in nineteenth-century St. Petersburg who has retired completely into what he calls the "underground," a state of total alienation and isolation from society. Severely misanthropic, the Underground Man believes himself to be more intelligent and perceptive than most other people in the world, but he also despises himself and frequently feels himself to be inferior or humiliated. We see all of the events and characters in the novel from the Underground Man's skewed perspective.

Liza A young prostitute whom the Underground Man tries to rescue after sleeping with her at a brothel. Liza is somewhat shy and innocent despite her profession, and she responds emotionally to the Underground Man's efforts to convince her of the error of her ways. She is naturally loving and sympathetic, but she also has a sense of pride and nobility.

Simonov A former schoolmate of the Underground Man, the only one with whom the Underground Man currently maintains a relationship. The Underground Man sees Simonov as an honest, independent man who is less narrow-minded than most people. Nonetheless, the Underground Man also suspects that Simonov despises him and finds his friendship burdensome.

Zverkov A friend of Simonov's and another former schoolmate of the Underground Man. Zverkov is a successful officer in the army and well liked by his friends. The Underground Man hated Zverkov during their school days, considering him to be coarse, boastful, and stupid. He is also jealous of Zverkov's wealth, confidence and popularity.

Ferfichkin Another of the Underground Man's former schoolmates and an admirer of Zverkov. In school, Ferfichkin was the Underground Man's "bitterest enemy." The Underground Man describes Ferfichkin as impudent, foolish, and cowardly, and notes that Ferfichkin frequently borrows money from Zverkov.

Trudolyubov Another former schoolmate of the Underground Man and a distant relation of Zverkov's. Trudolyubov is an honest man who treats the Underground Man with some degree of politeness. Nonetheless, he considers the Underground Man to be "nothing" and worships success of all kinds.

Apollon The Underground Man's elderly servant. Apollon lives with the Underground Man and performs household tasks for him somewhat grudgingly. The Underground Man thinks that Apollon is constantly judging him, and that he is unforgivably vain. The Underground Man hates the way Apollon looks and talks.

Anton Antonych Setochkin The head of Underground Man's department in the ministry. Anton Antonych is the closest thing to a friend that the Underground Man has. The Underground Man occasionally borrows money from Anton Antonych and visits his home on Tuesdays when he has an urge to be social.

The Officer A military officer who treats the Underground Man dismissively in a tavern one night, thereby making himself the object of the Underground Man's obsessive desire for revenge for several years. The Underground Man resents the officer for his rank, wealth, physical prowess, and confidence, but is also intimidated by him for these same reasons, and therefore can never make a move against him.

Analysis of Major Characters

The Underground Man

Dostoevsky says that the Underground Man, though a fictional character, is representative of certain people who "not only may but must exist in our society, taking under consideration the circumstances under which our society has generally been formed." The Underground Man is extremely alienated from the society in which he lives. He feels himself to be much more intelligent and "conscious" than any of the people he meets. However, he is aware that his consciousness often manifests itself as a skepticism that prevents him from having confidence in any of his actions. This skepticism cripples him and keeps him from participating in "life" as other people do. The Underground Man constantly analyzes and second-guesses every thought and feeling he has. He is therefore incapable of making decisions about anything.

Feeling himself to be inferior to more active, less intelligent people, the Underground Man goes through life full of shame and self-loathing. This feeling of inadequacy before others is enhanced by the fact that, as an orphan, he has never had normal, loving relationships with other people. Having no real life experiences upon which to base his hopes and expectations, he often relies on the conventions of novels and drama. The contrast between his expectations for life—which are based on literature—and the realities of the world he lives in is often great, and this divide alienates the Underground Man from society still further. The only emotional interactions he can have with others involve anger, bitterness, revenge, and humiliation. He can conceive of love only as the total domination of one person over another. In order to feel that he has participated in life in some way, he often instigates conflict with others and subjects himself to profound humiliation. This humiliation actually gives the Underground Man a sense of satisfaction and power, as he has brought about the humiliation himself. As long as he can exercise his will, he does not care if the outcome is positive or negative.

We meet the Underground Man when he is forty years old, having retired from his civil service job and secluded himself in a shabby apartment. By this point, he is a complete nihilist: he has no desire to interact with others, and he has total contempt for society and everyone who is part of it. In the second part of the novel, however, the Underground Man describes himself as he was sixteen years earlier, at the age of twenty-four. As a young man, the Underground Man is already misanthropic, proud, self-effacing, and bitter, but he also still clings to certain ideals. He is passionate about literature, craves human attention, and wants others to respect and admire him for his intelligence and passion. He is also occasionally subject to fits of idealism. In the course of the second part of the novel, however, we see how the Underground Man's inability to interact with other people causes his attempts to form relationships and participate in life to end in disaster, and drives him deeper underground.

LIZA

When Liza first appears in *Notes from Underground,* her function seems clear: she is the object of the Underground Man's latest literary fantasy and power trip. He has absorbed the literary archetype of the redeemed prostitute and has cast himself as the hero who will rescue Liza. Later in the novel, however, her character becomes more complex. When we first meet her, she matches the stereotype of a young prostitute: bored, jaded, and somewhat naïve. When Liza is genuinely moved by the Underground Man's speech, however, we realize that she may be even more innocent than expected. A young girl driven into prostitution by an uncaring family, she still idealizes romantic love and longs for respect and affection. She treasures the one declaration of love she has received, a note from a young medical student who does not know she is a prostitute. The Underground Man is touched by the fact that Liza so clearly treasures this letter, but his attitude toward her emotion is somewhat dismissive. We sense that Liza's sentiment could come from a less-educated version of the Underground Man's Romanticism and that her response to the Underground Man's speeches is shallow. Liza wants to participate in the artificial world the Underground Man creates with his "sentimental" speeches, because she likes the idea of being a romantic heroine instead of an ordinary prostitute.

When Liza responds tenderly and understandingly to the abusive speeches the Underground Man makes at his apartment, however, we see that she is closer to a real heroine than we may have expected. She is perceptive enough to see through the Underground Man's façade of cruelty and apathy, and she is good-hearted enough to try to give him comfort and love. When she finally realizes that the Underground Man is incapable of returning her love with anything but mockery and humiliation, she leaves with quiet strength and dignity. She throws away the wad of bills that the Underground Man gives her as "payment" for her visit, thwarting his attempt to treat her like a prostitute after she has come to him with help and love.

ZVERKOV

Zverkov is a prime example of the kind of man the Underground Man hates most, "*l'homme de la nature et de la vérité.*" Zverkov is an active and decisive man, preferring to pursue concrete goals rather than contemplate the value of those goals in modern society. He has been very successful, having advanced far in his career, seduced numerous women, and gained the admiration of his friends and acquaintances. In school, the Underground Man hated Zverkov for his stupidity and boastfulness, and resented him for his wealth, good looks, and popularity. The Underground Man explains that Zverkov was popular because he was "favored with the gifts of nature"—his social success was rather Darwinian. By the 1840s, Zverkov is much the same as he was in school, except a little fatter, probably because of his hearty enjoyment of food along with wine and women. The Underground Man feels that Zverkov treats him with condescension. The Underground Man is right, but Zverkov at least attempts to treat him politely. We see Zverkov, as we see all of the other characters in the novel, only through the eyes of the Underground Man. It is difficult, therefore, to get an objective view of Zverkov's real personality. The Underground Man describes Zverkov as a coarse, mincing, piggish idiot, but we can also see that Zverkov is amiable and generous with his friends. His rudeness to the Underground Man can be explained at least partially by the Underground Man's aggressive behavior.

Themes, Motifs & Symbols

Themes

Themes are the fundamental and often universal ideas explored in a literary work.

The Fallacies of Rationalism and Utopianism

Throughout the novel, the Underground Man makes a convincing case against the "rational egoists" and utopian socialists of his era, who claimed that the application of reason alone could perfect the world. Believing that destructive behavior results from a misguided sense of profit, these theorists thought that if everyone in the world understood what was really in their best interests, they would never do anything irrational or destructive. If the natural laws that governed human behavior could be understood, through reason, utopia would indeed be attainable.

The Underground Man opposes such a view because he believes that it underestimates the human desire for free will. He argues that humans value the ability to exert their own will—even if it runs contrary to their best interests—more than they value reason. The Underground Man's masochistic tendencies illustrate this theory. Rather than submit to the "law of reason" that dictates that only doctors and dentists can cure liver disease and toothaches, the Underground Man prefers to suffer his ailments in silence, even though this decision only brings him more pain. This example is absurd, almost parodic, but it emphasizes the Underground Man's point about human nature. Dostoevsky himself was highly suspicious of utopian socialists, worrying that their desire to codify rational human behavior ignored the complex nature of human beings. The freedom these utopian socialists preached could too easily lead to total uniformity—a uniformity that could lead to totalitarianism.

The Artificiality of Russian Culture

By the middle of the nineteenth century, the Russian social and intellectual elite had been imitating western European culture for decades. A nineteenth-century Russian man was considered "developed" and "educated" if he was familiar with the literary and philosophical traditions of Germany, France, and England. The Underground Man, with his intelligence, consciousness, and sense of the "beautiful and lofty" (a term borrowed from European philosophers Edmund Burke and Immanuel Kant), considers himself a "developed man of the nineteenth century." He tells us that, in his youth, he tried rather earnestly to live by the ideals he found in European literature and philosophy. Though Dostoevsky may have shared this fascination with European culture in his own youth, by the time he wrote *Notes from Underground,* he had decided that such pervasive European influence on Russia was destructive. Captivated by the West, Russian intellectuals had lost touch with the true Russian way of life the peasants and lower-class workers still practiced. To restore national unity and harmony, Dostoevsky called for a "return to the soil," emphasizing Russian values of family, religion, personal responsibility, and brotherly love over European "enlightenment," scientific progressivism, and utopianism. The Underground Man's European influences are partially responsible for driving him "underground," as his attempts to live by a foreign set of values meet with failure and frustration.

Paralysis of the Conscious Man in Modern Society

Throughout the novel we see that the Underground Man is unable to make decisions or take action with confidence. He explains that this inability is due to his intense degree of consciousness. The Underground Man is able to imagine the variety of consequences that every action could have, he is aware of the possible arguments that can be made against every statement, and he is conscious of the multiplicity of different motives that inform every decision he makes. As a result, the Underground Man sees that every choice a person makes is more complicated than it may seem on the surface. This complexity throws every decision into doubt. Action becomes impossible because it is impossible to determine the best course of action to take.

In earlier times, when religious and moral imperatives existed, people allayed any doubts about action and decision by following these imperatives in absolute confidence. In the modern era, however, most of these absolutes have dissolved. The only people who can act with confidence, according to the Underground Man, are narrow-minded people who are too stupid to question themselves.

The one remaining absolute, according to the Underground Man, is reason. Even educated men pursue the laws of science and reason without questioning them. The Underground Man—along with Dostoevsky himself—believes that such mindless adherence to the laws of reason is misguided. Dostoevsky does not necessarily believe, however, that total inaction is the best strategy for conscious people. He does believe, though, that an active person with a totally fixed mind—one that is not open to different possibilities—is more dangerous than an inactive person whose mind moves and changes.

Motifs

Motifs are recurring structures, contrasts, or literary devices that can help to develop and inform the text's major themes.

The Wet Snow

It always seems to be snowing in the world the Underground Man inhabits. The falling wet snow is more than simply an element of setting: the monotony of the weather and the dreariness of the snow echoes the changelessness and dreariness of the Underground Man's alienated life. The wet snow also serves to link the parts of the novel that take place in the 1860s (primarily Part I) with the parts that take place in the 1840s (primarily Part II). The Underground Man recalls the story of the dinner with Zverkov and his encounter with Liza because the same wet snow that fell on those days is falling as he composes his *Notes from Underground.*

L'Homme de la Nature et de la Vérité

The Underground Man is preoccupied with the idea of "*l'homme de la nature et de la vérité,*" which is French for "the man of nature and truth." The phrase is a distortion of a sentence from *Confessions* by the eighteenth-century French philosopher Jean-Jacques Rousseau. *Confessions* is a kind of autobiography meant to present a portrait of its author "exactly from nature and in all its truth." In *Notes from Underground,* this "man of nature and truth" becomes the "unconscious man," the man of action against whom the Underground Man opposes himself. This active man is healthy, single-minded—narrow-minded, according to the Underground Man—and acts according to the laws of nature and reason. The Underground Man disdains this type of man for his blind faith, yet he also feels inferior to such a man, considering himself a "mouse" or an "insect" in comparison.

Among the characters in the novel, Zverkov and the unnamed officer both share characteristics of *l'homme de la nature et de la vérité.*

The Redeemed Prostitute

The motif of the redeemed prostitute was popular in progressive novels, poems, and plays of the mid-nineteenth century. These works frequently involved variations on a standard plot: an altruistic hero rescues a young prostitute from a lifetime of degradation, using rhetoric to awaken the noble instincts that have been buried in her soul. In short, the hero appeals to the prostitute's sense of the "beautiful and lofty."

The Underground Man has absorbed this literary convention, and, wanting to imagine himself the hero of his own story, attempts to rescue the prostitute Liza. This attempt is an ironic one, however. First, it is symptomatic of the Underground Man's desire to "live out" literature in the real world. Moreover, the Underground Man is hardly an appropriate person to rescue anyone, as his own life is as miserable and empty as the lowliest prostitute's.

Symbols

Symbols are objects, characters, figures, or colors used to represent abstract ideas or concepts.

The Underground

The "underground," the "dark cellar" from which the Underground Man claims to be writing, is a symbol for his total isolation from society. He feels rejected and shut out from the society to which he is supposed to belong, and he imagines that he is viewing the world through cracks in the floorboards. The Underground Man often claims, however, to prefer the underground to the real world above. He treasures the space the underground gives him to exert his individuality—one of the few things he possesses.

St. Petersburg

The city of St. Petersburg serves as the backdrop for *Notes from Underground* and many of Dostoevsky's other works. The Underground Man makes frequent negative references to the city's climate, culture, and cost of living. His primary complaint is that the city is artificial: he describes it as an "abstract and intentional city," implying that nothing about the city feels natural or real. St. Petersburg is, in the Underground Man's eyes, rigidly systematized, bureaucratized, and alienating. St. Petersburg *is* an "artificial" city in a sense: it was built from scratch starting in 1703 by decree of Tsar Peter the Great, who hoped that the new city would become a "window on Europe." In 1713, St. Petersburg became the capital of Russia, but it never shook its origin as an artificial city. Peter the Great's desire to bring more European culture into Russia stimulated the Russian captivation with Western culture that Dostoevsky frequently criticized. For Dostoevsky, then, St. Petersburg is doubly artificial: not only was it built to order, but it also symbolizes the artificiality of the Russian adoption of European culture.

The Crystal Palace

The real Crystal Palace, a vast exhibition hall of glass and iron, was built in London for the Great Exhibition of 1851. The structure used the most advanced materials and technology available at the time. For progressive thinkers of the era, the idea of a crystal palace represented the ideal living space for a utopian society based on reason and natural laws. The Underground Man says he despises the idea of the crystal palace because he cannot stick his tongue out at it. By this he means that the blind, obstinate faith in reason that the crystal palace represents ignores the importance of individuality and personal freedom. However, the Underground Man seems to feel this way only about the crystal palace as envisioned by utopian thinkers, describing their palace as a "chicken coop" posing as a crystal palace. A real crystal palace would celebrate truth and harmony without reducing the complexities of human nature to confining mathematical laws, but the Underground Man cannot imagine its existence.

Money

For the Underground Man, money is a symbol of power. The Underground Man's poverty keeps him from feeling socially or even morally equal to others. He is deeply ashamed when he has to borrow money. In the few circumstances when the Underground Man attempts to exert his power, he is giving or withholding money. He tries to break Apollon's pride by withholding his wages, and he thrusts money into Liza's hands as she leaves his apartment in a deliberate attempt to assert that she is still nothing but a prostitute.

Summary & Analysis

Part I, Chapter I

Summary

The narrator—referred to in this SparkNote as the Underground Man—introduces himself. He describes himself as sick, wicked, and unattractive, and notes that he has a problem with his liver. He refuses to treat this ailment out of spite, although he understands that keeping his problems from doctors does the doctors themselves no harm.

The Underground Man explains that, during his many years in civil service, he was wicked, but that he considers this wickedness a kind of compensation for the fact that he never accepted bribes. He almost immediately revises this claim, however, admitting that he never achieved genuine wickedness toward his customers, but only managed to be rude and intimidating as a kind of game.

We learn that the Underground Man has retired early from his civil service job after inheriting a modest sum of money. He only held onto his low-ranking job so that he would be able to afford food, not because he got any satisfaction from it. He notes that he is filled with conflicting impulses: wickedness, sentimentality, self-loathing, contempt for others. His intense consciousness of these opposing elements has paralyzed him. He has settled into his miserable corner of the world, incapable of wickedness and incapable of action, loathing himself even as he congratulates himself on his own intelligence and sensitivity. He adds that the weather in St. Petersburg is probably bad for his health, but that he will stay there anyway, out of spite.

In a note to Chapter I included in some editions as an introduction to the novel, Dostoevsky explains his intention in writing *Notes from Underground*. He tells us that the author of the work is fictional, but notes that the nature of society makes it inevitable that people like this fictional narrator exist. As to the structure of the novel, Dostoevsky explains that in the first "fragment," entitled "Underground," the Underground Man introduces himself and explains "why he appeared and had to appear among us." The second half, entitled "Apropos of the Wet Snow," consists of the Underground Man's accounts of actual events in his life.

Analysis

The first chapter of *Notes from Underground* gives us a precise sketch of the Underground Man's character. By the end of the first paragraph, we get a sense of the issues that preoccupy the Underground Man. Contradictions and indecision are fundamental to his character. He says that his liver hurts, but then immediately tells us that he is not sure it is his liver. He knows he is sick, but he refuses to see a doctor out of spite, even though he knows that in pursuing this spiteful behavior he is only in hurting himself. He develops this idea of indecisive action later in the chapter, when he talks about the conflicts swarming inside him.

This inability to act stems from several important factors. First, the Underground Man is a nihilist, which means that he believes that traditional social values have no foundation in nature, and that human existence is essentially useless. The Underground Man despises the society in which he lives. Not only is the weather bad in St. Petersburg, but the culture of the city is built on bureaucracy and hypocrisy. Accepting bribes is common and widely tolerated. The Underground Man is filled with bitterness toward all aspects of society, but he is aware that he is powerless to act against it or within it. He cannot even manage to be a wicked civil servant. Instead, he takes his aggressions out on himself, refusing to see a doctor and remaining in an unhealthy climate out of spite. This behavior is the first evidence we have of the Underground Man's masochism, his enjoyment of his own pain and humiliation. The Underground Man explores this idea in more depth later in the novel.

Another important factor that contributes to the Underground Man's indecision is his intense self-consciousness. Though the Underground Man is frequently irrational, he is also extremely analytical and acutely conscious of every thought, urge, and feeling that crosses his mind. It is this heightened consciousness that makes him aware of all of the "opposite elements" inside him, so much so that he can never make a decision or act confidently on any of his desires.

The Underground Man is also highly conscious of what others think of him. He is intensely aware of our presence as readers. He addresses us frequently and directly, calling us "gentlemen," and he constantly analyzes and revises his statements in the fear that we are judging him. Indeed, the Underground Man treats us like a panel of hostile judges, looking down upon his underground life from our comfortable position above ground, from the vantage point of the social world he has fled.

Because we are aware that the Underground Man is conscious of our presence, we must question the validity of any statements he makes about not writing for our benefit. The Underground Man is a prime example of what is known in literaturc as an unreliable narrator: because everything we learn from the Underground Man is filtered though the lens of his own nihilistic, anguished perspective, we can never be sure he is telling us the objective truth about anything. We must use what we learn about the Underground Man's psychological state to fully understand his motives for telling us something, and to get a clear picture of the facts of his interactions with people.

Dostoevsky's note highlights the fact that the Underground Man is an unreliable narrator. By telling us that the Underground Man is fictional, and by describing the social conditions that might have produced someone like the Underground Man, Dostoevsky distances himself from his narrator. Because *Notes from Underground* is written in first person, it is easy to imagine that Dostoevsky and the Underground Man share the same perspective. However, one of the hallmarks of all of Dostoevsky's works is his ability to create distance between himself and his characters. One of the techniques he uses to accomplish this distance is humor. Indeed, in this novel, the Underground Man's behavior is so absurd that it often verges on the comic. Though Dostoevsky may share many of the Underground Man's opinions about society, he prefers to put those opinions in the mouth of someone rather unappealing and unconvincing. Dostoevsky feared that if he made his arguments too well, his readers would accept them without weighing their good and bad points.

The fact that the Underground Man is a civil servant is another important element. Many of Dostoevsky's most famous characters are low-ranking civil servants who are lost in the society of nineteenth century St. Petersburg. The Underground Man is just an average man, neither a philosopher nor a professional writer. As such, he does not use any philosophical terms when discussing his ideas. Although in his youth he was a great admirer of "the literary," by the time he is writing these notes, he has generally abandoned literary language, except in cases when he uses it ironically. Instead, the Underground Man uses everyday language with a kind of deliberate awkwardness.

Part I, Chapters II–IV

Summary: Chapter II

The Underground Man continues to describe himself. He is "overly conscious," a "developed man" who possesses far more consciousness than is necessary for survival in the nineteenth century. Narrow-minded, active people, in contrast, have the perfect amount of consciousness of reality to go about their daily lives. The Underground Man explains that he does not mean to deride these active figures by suggesting that they are not as conscious as he is, but then he immediately admits that he takes pride in his "sickness" of consciousness. He describes how his consciousness, which makes him aware of "everything beautiful and lofty," somehow inevitably drags him into corruption and "blight," a blight in which he has gradually learned to take a sick pleasure.

The end result of this consciousness is always inertia. The Underground Man believes that degradation is inherent in his nature and therefore impossible to change, which affords him a degree of satisfaction. Another kind of strangled satisfaction comes from the fact that the Underground Man, even though he despises himself, considers himself more intelligent than everyone around him, and therefore feels responsible for everything that happens to him. This sense of responsibility, of course, also increases his misery, and makes his pride in his own intelligence a source of shame.

Summary: Chapter III

The Underground Man further explains his inability to act in any directed fashion, whether magnanimously or vengefully. Once again, the problem is rooted in his self-consciousness. Normal men act immediately and blindly upon their instincts. In contrast to this kind of man, whom the Underground Man considers stupid but manly, the highly conscious Underground Man is nothing more than a mouse. While the normal man can perceive an act of revenge as an act of justice, the Underground Man, when wronged, is too conscious of the complexities of revenge to retaliate with genuine faith and confidence. Therefore, he ends up slinking back into his underground hole to dwell on whatever wrong has been done to him until it has almost consumed him.

A man of action follows his desire to act only until he is faced with definite impossibility, at which point he is reassured by the fact that further action will be useless. The Underground Man, however, claims that conscious men refuse to be reconciled with the laws of nature, science, and mathematics that other men take for granted. Even though the Underground Man is conscious of the reality of these laws, he refuses to agree with them if he does not like them.

Summary: Chapter IV

> *"Next you'll be finding pleasure in a toothache!" you will exclaim, laughing.*
> *"And why not? There is also pleasure in a toothache," I will answer.* (See QUOTATIONS, p. 57)

The Underground Man continues to illustrate the aesthetics of misery, demonstrating how the educated, conscious man of the nineteenth century can find pleasure even in a toothache. This pleasure comes from the unnecessary, almost artistically embellished moans and groans that the man uses to signal to his family and friends that he has a toothache, as well as from his awareness that his family is disgusted and irritated with his displays of agony. After making this argument, the Underground Man responds to the laughter that he imagines he has elicited from his audience, and explains that his jokes are in bad tone because he does not respect himself: "[H]ow can a man of consciousness have the slightest respect for himself?"

Analysis: Chapters II–IV

When the Underground Man implies that his great intelligence and heightened consciousness prevent him from being an "active man," saying that active people are always "disingenuous," he is rationalizing his inability to act. However, the fact that the Underground Man deludes himself about the source of his alienation does not mean that Dostoevsky necessarily wants to glorify the "man of action." Indeed, the novel criticizes equally those people who spend too much time contemplating the "beautiful and lofty" and those people who act decisively but blindly.

In Chapter II, the Underground Man essentially divides the world into two groups. The first group contains people who are both "disingenuous" and "active." These people are not necessarily stupid, but they are at most half as "conscious" as the Underground Man. Because they are unable to analyze every decision they make, they are able to make these decisions painlessly. They do not analyze obstacles any more than they analyze their own motives, so when they come to an obstacle they stop in their tracks without any concern. The second group that the Underground Man envisions contains educated, conscious people like him. These individuals spend all their time contemplating their own degradation.

This distinction between the two groups foreshadows the existentialist philosophy of writers like Jean-Paul Sartre, who considered *Notes from Underground* the first existentialist novel. Sartre believed that every human being is totally free and completely responsible for every choice he makes. In Sartre's work, those characters who become aware of the terrible responsibility that accompanies every choice they make often are unable to bring themselves to do anything. Like the narrow-minded men in the first of the Underground Man's two groups, the only people who act with total confidence in Sartre's works are those who are not conscious of their freedom and responsibility. Nonetheless, Sartre believes that the conscious man *must* act, however little the idea appeals to him.

It may seem odd that the Underground Man aligns the laws of science and mathematics with the less intelligent men, as we usually think of those disciplines as requiring education and intelligence. However, for the Underground Man, a conscious man is someone who questions and analyzes everything, even the validity of so-called natural laws. Someone who has blind faith in everything, even in logic and reason, fits the Underground Man's definition of an unconscious man. This definition allows the Underground Man to include some of the most prominent intellectuals of the era in his criticism, and paves the way for his upcoming critique of the "rational" theorists in Chapter VII.

Of course, the Underground Man considers his consciousness a curse even as he takes pride in it. This masochistic idea becomes literal when he discusses the pleasure that a cultured man can find in a toothache. Though the Underground Man is ashamed of this pleasure, as he is ashamed of anything he finds enjoyable or worthy of pride, he believes it is the only kind of pleasure available to the truly developed man in the nineteenth century. This moment is one of several instances in the novel when Dostoevsky's message likely differs from the Underground Man's: we see the toothache as an example of the absurdity that arises when intelligence and sensitivity are unaccompanied by action.

Part I, Chapters V–VIII

Summary: Chapter V

> *[P]erhaps I really regard myself as an intelligent man only because throughout my entire life I've never been able to start or finish anything.*
>
> (See QUOTATIONS, p. 58)

The Underground Man describes his occasional bouts of repentance, tenderheartedness, and sentimentality. He feels these emotions frequently, and imagines that he is feeling them sincerely. However, he always ends up convincing himself that these moments are nothing but affectations and delusions. He explains that all of the emotional torment he has undergone in his life has been the result of boredom. In an attempt to make his life into something he could "live, at least somehow, a little," he convinces himself that someone has offended him, or forces himself to fall in love. These ineffectual gestures toward living are the Underground Man's compensation for the inertia his consciousness imposes upon him.

The Underground Man repeats his earlier point that only narrow-minded people can be truly active, because their lack of consciousness allows them the comforting belief that there are absolute principles upon which they can base their actions. The Underground Man, in contrast, has nothing solid to support his actions, not even pure wickedness. He analyzes his actions until the idea of cause and effect dissolves. Moreover, the Underground Man also overanalyzes his rebellions against this inertia—his blind attempts at love or anger—until he hates himself for forcing false emotions, and therefore feels paralyzed and becomes more inert than ever. He feels he is an intelligent man only because he has never been able to start or finish anything. In this regard, his inertia is a mark of his consciousness.

Summary: Chapter VI

The Underground Man describes the difference between inertia and laziness. He defines laziness as a positive quality: a lazy person can be identified positively as a "lazybones," whereas the Underground Man is identifiable only by qualities that he lacks. The Underground Man imagines himself as a "lazybones": he would spend all his time drinking to the health of everything "beautiful and lofty," and would convince himself that everything, even the ugliest things in the world, were "beautiful and lofty" so that he could drink even more. He would demand respect for his opinions and die in peace, extremely fat and "positive" from all of his drinking and eating, a "positive" in a "negative age."

SUMMARY: CHAPTER VII

The Underground Man attempts to debunk the mid-nineteenth-century progressive idea that man, if he were to understand his own true interests clearly, would never do anything bad because it is most advantageous to him to behave rationally. The Underground Man, in contrast, believes that man consciously acts to his own disadvantage, simply to be obstinate. He questions the meaning of the word "advantage," claiming that utilitarian theorists derived their list of advantages—prosperity, wealth, freedom, peace—from statistical figures and politico-economic formulas. The Underground Man suggests that there is one "strange advantage," which he will explain later, that evades these classifications. This "strange advantage" explains why an enlightened man may suddenly and perversely act against what appears to be his own advantage.

The Underground Man goes on to claim that the rules of logic can never predict human behavior. He mentions the English historian Henry Thomas Buckle's theory that civilization gradually softens men, making them incapable of waging war. This theory, while logically sound, is disproved by the fact that more blood has been shed in the ostensibly civilized nineteenth century than in more barbaric times.

The Underground Man predicts that man would grow bored in a society based on scientifically derived formulas for moral behavior. In the end, "ungrateful" men would welcome the chance to overturn logic and live according to their own irrational free will. The Underground Man thinks that man, under any circumstance, prefers to think he is acting as he *wants* to act, not as reason dictates. The "strange advantage" mentioned earlier is complete free will—even the choice to do something self-destructive. The most important thing to man is that his freedom of choice not be constrained by anything—even reason.

Summary: Chapter VIII

Who wants to want according to a little table?
(See QUOTATIONS, p. 59)

The Underground Man responds to his imagined audience's claim that free will is something that can be explained scientifically, just as every other human urge can be. He argues that science, regardless of what it might discover about the human will, cannot change the fact that man refuses to accept that his free will is subject to rules. Man, he contends, will do anything to demonstrate this independence of will. The only constants in man's behavior are that he is ungrateful and refuses to be sensible. Man may even intentionally go insane, simply to prove that his free will is not subject to reason and that he may behave irrationally if he so desires.

Analysis: Chapters V–VIII

This section addresses the tension between the ideologies of the sentimental and idealistic 1840s, when the Underground Man was a young man, and the more utilitarian and scientific 1860s, the time in which he is writing *Notes from Underground.* The Underground Man displays a mixture of contempt and longing for the ideal of genuine love. He displays the same conflicted attitude toward the sublime literature of the Enlightenment and Romantic periods, when everyone from the philosopher Immanuel Kant to the writer Victor Hugo celebrated the "beautiful and lofty." The Underground Man is clearly familiar with the major writers of these periods, as he makes references throughout the novel to works by the French novelists Victor Hugo and Georges Sand, the English poet Lord Byron, and the Russian Romantics Aleksandr Pushkin and Mikhail Lermontov. The Underground Man's attempts to "live a little" are, in a sense, attempts to experience the powerful emotions that the Romantic writers valued. Though the Underground Man prides himself on his ability to recognize the "beautiful and lofty," his disgust with himself and with society has crushed any faith he may have had in Romantic ideals. As a result, he feels disgusted with himself whenever he feels strong emotions, and he mocks the idea of the "beautiful and lofty" when he imagines himself as an alcoholic aesthete-lazybones in Chapter VI.

The 1860s in Europe were marked by an increased interest in social reform based on scientific principles. Utopian thinkers believed that life could be perfected solely through the application of reason and enlightened self-interest. Any serious problems remaining in the world existed only because the scientific method for getting rid of them had not yet been discovered. One of the most prominent Russian proponents of these ideas was N. G. Chernyshevsky, who developed the theory of "rational egoism" and wrote a revolutionary novel called *What Is to Be Done?* in 1863. Dostoevsky, contemptuous of Chernyshevsky's theories, frequently attacks and parodies the theorist's ideologies throughout *Notes from Underground.* Among Chernyshevsky's ideas, Dostoevsky found his theories of "rational egoism" particularly offensive. A character in *What Is to Be Done?* asserts that, in following his own desires, he will make other people happy; he ends with the question "Do you hear that, you, in your underground hole?" In many ways, *Notes from Underground* is the response from that underground hole, a long protest against the idea that a man must be happy merely because others want him to be.

The Underground Man resists the idea of rational egoism, believing man to be an inherently irrational creature. Man will always try to assert his free will, even if asserting this free will goes against reason and self-interest. The Underground Man believes so because he can think of no other explanation for the way others have treated him in his life. If human nature were inherently good, no one could ever act the way most people act toward him. However, the Underground Man, as he mentions in Chapter I, would prefer to have a rotting liver than bend to a doctor's authority. He is clearly obsessed with free will, and seems to project this obsession onto others.

In these chapters, the Underground Man continues to use his intelligence as an excuse for his inactivity, and his inactivity as proof of his intelligence. He considers active men universally "dull and narrow-minded"—the very traits that allow them to act. In contrast, the Underground Man's supreme intelligence does not permit him to assuage any of the doubts that encumber action. Every question that he begins to resolve presents him with new, unanswerable questions. In earlier chapters, he says that intelligence necessarily results in inactivity, but now he implies that inactivity is in itself an indication of intelligence. The Underground Man claims that it is possible that he only considers himself intelligent because he has "never been able to start or finish anything."

Conversely, the Underground Man sees action as an indication of low intelligence. In Chapter VI, when he imagines himself as a "positive" man whose life has some kind of goal, the image that he creates is parodic and absurd. The goal he imagines for himself is the celebration of everything "beautiful and lofty," and the image he creates—of a man with indiscriminate but strongly held opinions—is laughable. This example illustrates what happens when we place too much value on opinion for opinion's sake. Taken in the context of the Underground Man's comments about his own intelligence, it can also be read as a commentary on decisiveness in general. Indeed, the Underground Man's main criticism of the rational theorists in Chapter VII is that they have chosen a system and decided to stick by it. These theorists' refusal to allow the possibility that their laws are fallible puts them, in the Underground Man's eyes, on par with the stupidest man in the world.

Part I, Chapters IX–XI

Summary: Chapter IX

The Underground Man suddenly implies that everything he has said in the last few chapters has all been a bitter joke. Nonetheless, he continues to wonder if it is in man's best interest to act for his own profit. He admits that man feels a compulsion to create, but that he feels an equally strong urge to destroy. Animals delight in the creations they have made, as ants delight in an anthill they have built. Man, on the other hand, takes pleasure only in the creative *process,* never in its end result. Man senses that after he fully achieves all of his goals, there will be nothing left to do, and so he fears that achievement. To man, then, the full illumination that logic offers is alarming.

Then the Underground Man wonders whether suffering is not just as valuable to mankind as the well-being achieved through the use of reason. He states that suffering is the cause of consciousness. Though he has complained about consciousness before, he thinks that consciousness surpasses reason. Reason may solve all the world's problems, but then man is left with nothing to do. Consciousness renders man immobile, but allows him to "occasionally whip" himself, which at least "livens things up a bit."

Summary: Chapter X

The Underground Man mocks the utopian fascination with the idea of the crystal palace, an indestructible edifice that epitomizes rationality. He fears the crystal palace because he is unable to stick his tongue out at it. He then mentions that if the palace were a chicken coop, he would use it for shelter, but never call it a palace. If he desired a crystal palace, he would refuse to accept anything less—such as the mundane accomodations of city life—than that palace. If no one pays attention to his desires, he always has the underground.

Suddenly, the Underground Man wants us to forget that he rejected the crystal palace. He wonders if he was only upset because he has nothing at which to stick out his tongue. He wonders why he desires things like crystal palaces when he should be content with apartments, thinking his desire might be some cruel hoax. He then remarks that those who live underground like him never stop talking once they start, even though they have been silent for years.

Summary: Chapter XI

The last chapter of the "Underground" section of the novel begins with the Underground Man's resolution that the "conscious inertia" of the underground surpasses the life of the normal man. Nonetheless, he continues to envy the normal man bitterly. In the next moment, he declares that he is lying, and that in fact he believes nothing of what he has written so far, even if at the time he thought that he believed it. This statement is followed by a long speech by the Underground Man's imagined, outraged audience, who chastises him for his inconsistency, his lack of integrity, his cowardice in refusing to stand by any of his statements, and his general depravity.

The Underground Man responds that he has made up the audience's entire speech. He wonders if the audience is "indeed so gullible" as to think that he will publish his notes and allow them to be read. Then he wonders why he addresses the audience at all when he does not plan to let them read the notes. He explains that the notes are his attempt to confront those memories and thoughts that he has trouble revealing even to himself. Addressing an audience is merely a formal construction to help him to write. He decides that perhaps he uses this imaginary audience because he is a coward, or else in order to "behave more decently" while writing.

As for why he writes at all, the Underground Man finds writing to be a cathartic experience, allowing him some relief from his nagging memories. It also relieves his boredom and makes him feel like he is doing something productive. He then introduces the next part of *Notes from Underground*: the dull, wet snow he sees falling outside his window reminds him of an anecdote from his past that he cannot forget, so he decides to tell his story "apropos of the wet snow."

Analysis: Chapters IX–XI

The Underground Man's discussion of the creative and destructive instincts of humankind is closely related to the nature of the society in which he lives. During the time the Underground Man was a civil servant in St. Petersburg, he faced a burdensome, pointless bureaucracy in his day-to-day existence. Furthermore, in various parts of the novel he has commented on the city's artificiality. In this regard, *Notes from Underground* is the forerunner of a slew of literary works about the human condition in the modern era, many of them expressing similar concerns about the alienating effect modern bureaucratic existence has on the common man. Whereas preindustrial man engaged in a constant physical struggle to stay alive, producing tools that were directly related to his survival, postindustrial man does work that has no direct connection to his daily physical needs. He does not see the results of his labor and feels alienated him from his work. Advances in technology only assure that there will be less for man to do and achieve. As a result, the boredom of modern life makes suffering into a kind of diversion or release. Dostoevsky was fully aware of this sense of alienation in postindustrial man, and he supported a somewhat conservative movement that emphasized the importance of community, religion, and personal responsibility in combating this alienation. The name of this conservative movement translates as "Back to the Soil," implying a rejection of the postindustrial society to which the Underground Man belongs.

The crystal palace was an important symbol for the progressive thinkers and utilitarians of the 1860s. Chernyshevsky imagined a crystal palace as an ideal living space for his utopian society, basing its structure on the real-life Crystal Palace that was shown in London at the Great Exhibition of 1851, which Dostoevsky saw during a trip to Europe. The Crystal Palace at the Exhibition, built entirely of glass and cast iron, represented the height of modern building technology. Clear as crystal, made with modern methods, and constructed entirely with modern materials, the Palace embodied the values of rational egoism, liberal socialism, and utilitarianism that the Underground Man derides in the later chapters of

"Underground." When the Underground Man says that he despises anything at which he cannot stick out his tongue, he is imagining the physical embodiment of progressive and utopian theories. If the imaginary crystal palace represents the triumph of reason over disorder, sticking out his tongue represents the Underground Man's determination to prevent reason from overcoming his obstinate free will.

Even though the Underground Man begins Chapter X by deriding the utilitarians' crystal palace, he suddenly insinuates that the palace represents everything he desires but can never have. This odd twist can be explained by the fact that the chapter was severely censored before it was published. Dostoevsky later claimed that the omitted passages expressed an idea central to the entire novel—the need for religion and faith. Indeed, in the second half of Chapter X, the Underground Man speaks with more feeling and conviction than he uses elsewhere, suddenly clinging to an idealism that he says he will never abandon. These passages suggest that he rejects Chernyshevsky's crystal palace not because of its perfection but because it tries to pass off something banal, ordinary, and limiting (such as a chicken coop) as a palace. Chernyshevsky's philosophy is flawed because it neglects the freedom of the human will. The Underground Man will only accept a utopia that offers man all of the "advantages" he needs, even though such a utopia is impossible to imagine. Inevitably, though, the Underground Man rejects this idealism at the end of the chapter. At the beginning of Chapter XI, the Underground Man recovers his bitter and contradictory nature, saying, "[L]ong live the underground!" and then immediately revising that comment to "Devil take the underground!" We see yet again that he refuses to make a genuine ideological statement.

At the end of "Underground," the Underground Man offers a reasonably in-depth analysis of his own psyche and the motives that are compelling him to write. He also addresses his need to behave as though he has an audience of judges even though he plans never to publish his manuscript. This somewhat convoluted and tangled analysis is ahead of its time. Though Dostoevsky wrote long before Freud, *Notes from Underground* tackles the psychological complexity of its main character with an awareness and depth previously unknown in nineteenth-century literature. Now that we have such a deep sense of the Underground Man's character, as "Apropos of the Wet Snow" opens we are given the opportunity to see how those character traits work in the social world.

Part II, Chapter I

Summary

The Underground Man begins his narration of events that occurred when he was twenty-four years old. Even at that young age, he is already depressed and antisocial. At work, he never looks anyone in the eye, and he imagines that they look at him with disgust. He vacillates between despising everyone he knows because they are dull-witted and feeling intensely inferior to them. He always feels alienated, conscious of how different he is from everyone else. Occasionally, he grows suddenly indifferent to his problems, becomes briefly chummy with his coworkers, and attributes his usual "intolerance and fastidiousness" to Romanticism.

In a digression from this retrospective narrative, the Underground Man discusses the nature of Russian Romanticism, which he claims is not "translunary" like German or French Romanticism. Russian Romanticism is "to see everything, and to see often incomparably more clearly than our very most positive minds do." Generally, the Russian form of Romanticism is open-minded and practical, concerned with the preservation of "the beautiful and lofty" but also with an eye for self-preservation. The Russian Romantic does not seem to let his Romanticism get in the way of his career: he "wouldn't lift a finger for his ideal" yet believes in this ideal steadfastly. He is at once "loftily honest" and a "scoundrel."

After this explanation, the Underground Man returns to his earlier narrative. At the age of twenty-four, he needs external stimulation to stifle his inner turmoil, and the only external stimulation he can bear is reading. Sometimes he feels the need for "contradictions, contrasts," and he engages in timid, shameful debaucheries. Afraid of being seen, he frequents shadowy, disreputable places.

One night, after seeing someone thrown out a tavern window in a fight, he desires a fight himself. These attempts are thwarted, however. Rather than fight with the Underground Man, an officer he meets casually shoves him aside. The Underground Man does not protest, even though he is not afraid of the physical damage that the officer could inflict on him. Rather, he lacks the "moral courage" to challenge the officer. The Underground Man, as a romantic, would use "literary language" with the officer, and he understands that the people in the tavern would humiliate him for doing so.

Rather than challenge the officer, the Underground Man becomes obsessed with the idea of revenge. He stalks the officer and gathers casual information about him. However, whenever the Underground Man sees the officer walking in the park, he gives way, so that the officer does not even notice his presence. Finally, the Underground Man decides that his revenge will come in refusing to give way to the officer, because then the officer will have to acknowledge his existence.

The Underground Man spends a long time preparing for this confrontation, resorting to borrowing money to purchase quality clothing—a hat, gloves, a shirt, and a fur collar—so that he will look like the officer's social equal. Even dressed in his fine clothes, however, the Underground Man cannot bring himself to bump into the officer. One day, he finally succeeds in walking straight into the officer, but the officer does not even seem to notice. At first, the Underground Man exults that he has placed himself on equal footing with the officer and preserved his own dignity. Three days later, however, he feels the same shame he feels after every debauch. The Underground Man wonders what became of the officer: "Whom does he crush now?"

Analysis

The first chapter of "Apropos of the Wet Snow" reveals a good deal about the Underground Man's experience with and attitude toward literature, particularly the Romantic literature written in and before the 1840s. We learn that the Underground Man has been an avid reader all his life, and that reading is one of the few pursuits and situations with which he feels comfortable. The Underground Man admires "literary language" and wishes that he inhabited a society where that kind of language was part of daily interactions.

The Underground Man's relationship with literature, however, is highly ambiguous. He is ashamed of the "romanticism" that leads him to want to befriend his coworkers. Though he seems to admire the Russian brand of Romanticism, he also describes it as somewhat hypocritical and absurd. Dostoevsky himself disapproved of the degree to which Russian intellectuals of his time adopted western European culture and ideals. As the Underground Man explains in his description of Russian Romantics, the "translunary" qualities of French and German Romanticism do not translate to the Russian version of Romanticism, which is too practical and honest. Though the Underground Man is conscious enough to understand this difference, he does not necessarily understand that many of the qualities that he admires in literature—and that he subsequently attempts to transfer to his own life—are European and untranslatable. He knows that the soldiers from the tavern will not accept a duel and will laugh at his use of "literary language," but he attributes this to their lack of intelligence and sensitivity.

Dostoevsky believed that European culture had been artificially imposed upon Russian culture. The Underground Man believes that he should live by European cultural rules, so he attempts to apply them to life in Russia—a project that Dostoevsky believes can only lead to frustration and failure. Though European culture is alien to Russia, it has replaced Russian culture in places like St. Petersburg. The city is an artificial place—the Underground Man calls it "intentional and abstract" —with no natural culture of its own, supporting an artificial, untranslatable culture that can only alienate its inhabitants.

The Underground Man's interaction with the soldier, however pathetic it may appear, has its roots in Romantic European ideas of justice and revenge. The Underground Man wants to walk with the officer as an equal, but when he tries to put this progressive idea into practice, he fails. The confrontation with the officer is a parody of a similar passage in Chernyshevsky's novel *What Is to Be Done?* Dostoevsky implies that literature, however rational, cannot supply its readers with a model for living. The Underground Man's desire for the officer to throw him out of the window indicates the degree to which the Underground Man is starved for any social interaction. He is so alienated that he craves *any* interaction, regardless of whether that interaction is positive or negative. The Underground Man's failure to achieve a satisfying interaction with the officer is typical of his inability to ever achieve human contact on conventional terms. His behavior with the officer is just as he describes it in "Underground": he wants to act, but resists the urge and spends months obsessing over the offense before finally exacting a limited, anticlimactic, and pathetic revenge.

Part II, Chapter II

Summary

After the initial sense of his victory wears off, the Underground Man becomes nauseated and repentant, just as he described in "Underground." To escape these unpleasant feelings, he retreats into intense, rapturous dreams in which he becomes a noble hero. All his mockery dissolves in "faith, hope, and love," and he imagines that wonderful opportunities for activity will present themselves to him.

Sometimes, flashes of the "beautiful and lofty" come upon the Underground Man in the middle of his debauches, and he says that the contrast between these flashes of loftiness and the degradation of his debauches creates a delicious suffering. In his dreams he feels love, though he feels no need to apply the love to his real life. His dreams always end with artistic moments stolen from poetry and novels. He describes the scenes of his dreams: they combine elements from the life of Napoleon and from Lord Byron's *Manfred*, a poem about a proud and gloomy hero. The Underground Man imagines that his audience considers vulgar, and he is ashamed of himself for needing to justify his own dreams.

After three months of dreaming, the ecstasy of his dreams makes the Underground Man want to embrace mankind. He feels the need to "rush into society." His only social outlet is the chief of his department, Anton Antonych Setochkin. On Tuesdays, the Underground Man can drink tea at Setochkin's house with Setochkin's two daughters and one or two other guests. At tea, the Underground Man invariably becomes paralyzed, incapable of participating in conversation. When he goes home, though, he feels he has been cured of his need for social interaction for a while.

One Thursday, the Underground Man becomes too lonely to wait until the following Tuesday and decides to visit a former classmate, Simonov. Although the Underground Man considered his time at school "penal servitude" and has cut off relations with most of his classmates, he believes that Simonov is less narrow-minded and more honest than the others, and therefore maintains a relationship with him. The Underground Man suspects that he disgusts Simonov, but he is not sure.

ANALYSIS

The subject matter of the Underground Man's dreams is further evidence that he has fully absorbed the European literary and cultural models that Dostoevsky believed were artificially imposed upon Russia. The figures with which the Underground Man identifies his "heroic" self come from French and English history and literature: many of the details and imagery of his great dreams come from the life of Napoleon, while others are related to the fictional Manfred from Lord Byron's poem. These dreams show us that the Underground Man is capable of genuine emotion and pleasure: he describes the dreams as "sweet" and refuses to dismiss them. However, his expression of these pleasant feelings is misdirected. Rather than share his feelings with others, the Underground Man expresses them in imaginary situations, using the imagery of an alien culture—that of western Europe. His fantasies, then, have no place in the world in which he lives. The Underground Man's dreams function as an allegory for the irrelevancy of Western culture imposed on Russian lives. The dreams also indicate that the Underground Man's real life has been so devoid of satisfying human interaction that he can only find models for happiness and triumph in literature.

The Underground Man does, of course, have urges to interact socially with other human beings. These urges come after several months of "dreaming." After immersing himself in a world modeled on literature rather than real life, he feels that he is capable of interacting with people. Comfortable in the realm of the literary and in the landscape of his own imagination, the Underground Man is able to convince himself that he is capable of participating in the real social world. Moreover, his sizable ego drives him to want to share his wonderful thoughts and feelings with the rest of the world. This urge to socialize also reveals that the twenty-four-year-old Underground Man is not yet entirely entrenched in the underground—he wants to interact with the outside world.

The fact that the Underground Man can only visit Setochkin on Tuesdays, and therefore must limit and schedule his desires for social interaction, is another indicator of the artificiality of the Underground Man's environment. We can understand how people living in St. Petersburg might feel frustrated and alienated like the Underground Man when they discover that even natural, human impulses toward companionship are regulated, programmed, and bureaucratized. When the Underground Man overcomes his social problems enough to try to take action, society and convention thwart him—the very society and convention that are, at least in part, responsible for his social problems from the start.

PART II, CHAPTER III

SUMMARY

The Underground Man arrives at Simonov's apartment to find Simonov with two other former schoolmates. They are discussing plans for a farewell dinner for Zverkov, another former schoolmate who is now an officer in the army. The Underground Man remembers Zverkov as one of his least favorite classmates. He was handsome, confident, wealthy, and popular. The Underground Man considered Zverkov vulgar, and hated Zverkov's boasting about his future successes with women and in duels.

Zverkov has had success in the army and with women ever since he left school, and he no longer greets the Underground Man on the street. Simonov's two guests are both admirers of Zverkov: Ferfichkin, an "enemy" of the Underground Man from school who often borrows money from Zverkov; and Trudolyubov, whom the Underground Man considers honest but too focused on success. Although all three men essentially ignore the Underground Man from the moment he enters the room, he insists on being included in the farewell dinner, feeling that an offer to contribute money for the meal will make the other men respect him. Simonov hesitates, irritated with the Underground Man, but ultimately allows him to join the dinner. When the other men leave, Simonov invents an excuse and says that he must run off. The Underground Man awkwardly leaves the apartment.

After leaving, the Underground Man regrets everything he has just done. He knows that he is not wanted at the dinner, he hates Zverkov, and he does not have enough money to pay for the meal. However, he knows that he will still go to the dinner: the more inappropriate it is for him to go, the more likely it is that he will go. He decides to spend the money that he owes Apollon, his servant, on dinner.

That night, the Underground Man remembers his time at school. He was an orphan, and distant relatives sent him to a school where the other students derided him because he was different from them. He hated the other children, who were narrow-minded, worshiped only success, and mocked "everything that was just." Their faces grew more stupid with every year spent at school. Hoping to avoid their mockery, the Underground Man became one of the best students at the school. He impressed the others with his knowledge of books and the respect he gained from his teachers. He made one friend among his classmates, but he treated the friend tyrannically. When the friend's will was broken, the Underground Man pushed him away. After he left school the Underground Man broke all ties with his former life. He even abandoned the "special service" for which he had been trained, in order to pursue a humbler career.

The Underground Man spends the next day dreading and preparing for the dinner. He imagines it will somehow prove to be a turning point in his life. He examines his shabby wardrobe and discovers a spot on his trousers that will make him look undignified in the eyes of his dinner companions. He imagines the other men's disdain in elaborate detail, despairing that his predicament will be so banal and "non-literary." Still, the Underground Man wants to prove to the others that he is not a coward. He entertains fantasies in which he wins over all of his former classmates with his wit and intelligence. At the same time, he maintains that none of his worries are important at all. He passes the day in nervous agony until his "wretched little wall clock hisse[s] five," at which point he spends his last fifty kopecks on a coach to take him to dinner.

Analysis

In the Underground Man's description of Zverkov we see the model for his later discussions of the active but stupid man. The Underground Man has no respect for Zverkov, believing him to be arrogant and dull-witted, but he is aware that Zverkov's confidence has won him many accomplishments, as well as friends and admirers. The Underground Man fantasizes about Zverkov admiring the Underground Man's brilliance and sensitivity and offering himself in friendship, and he reveals an intense desire to be liked and accepted by the men he disdains most. This desire is colored by the Underground Man's egoism—he can only imagine being admired, not simply accepted or liked—and his lack of experiences outside of books. As always, the Underground Man's fantasy takes a highly "literary" form, involving dramatic and literary conventions.

The account of the Underground Man's time at school helps to explain his bitterness. An orphan who was always too sensitive and antisocial to win much love or affection at school, the Underground Man has gone through life unloved. His relationship with his one friend at school shows us that, even as a young person, he had no idea how to conduct a real relationship. He does not understand love or faith, only domination and submission. He craves power because all his life he has had to stand by in impotent rage and submit to the will of stronger and more powerful people.

Two manifestations of the Underground Man's masochism appear in this chapter. We learn that the Underground Man quit his lucrative and prestigious career in civil service simply out of spite, just as he now refuses to go to the doctor out of spite. Moreover, the Underground Man decides to go to the dinner for Zverkov even though he clearly is not wanted, partially because of an inexplicable desire to plunge himself into uncomfortable situations. The Underground Man imagines that these situations are the only way for him to experience real life. Indeed, as we have noticed, his only emotional interchanges with others involve anger, hate, and discomfort. He believes these uncomfortable sensations to be strongly tied to any kind of social behavior.

The Underground Man continues to be obsessed with external appearances, just as he was when he plotted his revenge on the officer. The Underground Man frets because of the shabby condition of his clothes, particularly his stained pair of trousers, imagining that the four friends at the restaurant will look down on him because of his slovenly appearance. Though this concern is not wholly unfounded, it reveals that the Underground Man sees the world—not just the readers of his memoirs—as a panel of judges. For the Underground Man, external appearances and the meanings they conceal are often one and the same. At the end of the chapter, the wall clock "hisse[s]" five o'clock. The Underground Man's use of such a negative word to describe the sounds of a clock indicates that he projects his discontent onto the world around him. These word choices remind us that we should be careful about accepting any information the Underground Man gives us—he likely observes all people and objects with the same distorted hatred he applies to the wall clock.

Part II, Chapters IV–V

Summary: Chapter IV

The Underground Man arrives at the Hotel de Paris twenty-five minutes after dinner is supposed to begin, but he is the first to arrive. Discovering that Simonov has ordered dinner for six o'clock rather then five o'clock, he waits awkwardly in the restaurant, imagining that he is disgraced in the eyes of the waiters. When Zverkov arrives with the other dinner guests, he treats the Underground Man condescendingly. The Underground Man is appalled that Zverkov might genuinely consider himself superior to him. The other guests treat the Underground Man with awkward politeness, although they make derisive comments about his income and appearance. The Underground Man explodes at them, insisting that he is not embarrassed and that he will be paying for his dinner himself. The others are annoyed, and Trudolyubov insinuates that the Underground Man is an unwanted guest.

Feeling "crushed and annihilated," the Underground Man sits down and drinks sherry in silence as the others laugh and talk. He resents them and plans to leave. After a while, he delivers an offensive and pointless speech to Zverkov. Ferfichkin responds with a threat of violence, and the Underground Man challenges him to a duel. The others laugh, noting that the Underground Man is drunk. Once again, the Underground Man falls silent and tries to look indifferent and disinterested. Secretly, however, he wishes he could make peace with the other men.

The Underground Man watches the others drinking and making ridiculous conversation. He paces loudly back and forth in the dining room for three hours, but the other dinner guests ignore him. He considers how much he has humiliated himself, thinking about how the others do not understand how developed and sensitive he is. When they do address a comment to him, the Underground Man guffaws disdainfully.

At eleven o'clock the other men make a move to leave. The Underground Man begs Ferfichkin's forgiveness, insisting that if they duel, he will give Ferfichkin the first shot and then fire into the air. The men answer him with contempt and leave together, planning to go to a brothel. The Underground Man insists that Simonov lend him six roubles so that he can accompany them. Simonov responds with scorn, but finally flings the money at the Underground Man and leaves. The Underground Man decides that if he cannot make the men beg for his friendship, he will slap Zverkov's face.

Summary: Chapter V

> *Here it is, here it is at last, the encounter with reality. . . . All is lost now!*
>
> (See QUOTATIONS, p. 60)

The Underground Man hires a peasant coachman to take him to the brothel where the others have gone, convinced that he can redeem himself by slapping Zverkov. In the coach, he imagines the events at the brothel: he will slap Zverkov and everyone will retaliate by beating him—even Olympia the prostitute, who once laughed in the Underground Man's face. Eventually, Zverkov will have to duel with the Underground Man. The Underground Man accepts that he will lose his job, and tries to figure out how he will pay for pistols and find a second for his duel. He does not have any close friends who will act as second, but he thinks that anyone he asks will be honor-bound to accept. He urges the coachman to go faster, but he is plagued by doubt.

If Zverkov refuses to duel, the Underground Man will bite him and allow himself to be sent to Siberia in disgrace. Years later, he will return from Siberia and nobly forgive Zverkov for his dishonor. The Underground Man then realizes that he has stolen this fantasy from the plot of popular Romantic stories. In despair, he considers turning back, but decides it is his fate to go on. He hits the coachman in the neck with impatience. As the carriage continues through the falling snow, the Underground Man feels that slapping Zverkov has become inevitable.

When the Underground Man arrives at the brothel, where he has been before, he finds the drawing room empty. He realizes that the others have already gone off with various women. He paces the room, trying to decide what to do until a young prostitute with a kind, serious face appears in the room. She appeals to the Underground Man, who decides to sleep with her. He notices his bedraggled appearance in a mirror and decides that he does not care if she finds him repulsive. In fact, he would rather she did.

Analysis: Chapters IV–V

The Underground Man's description of his wait at the restaurant mirrors his description of the hissing wall clock: just as he imagines that the inanimate clock is hostile, he imagines that the waiters performing their tasks are full of contempt for him, and he is ashamed. Every casual occurrence, from the late arrival of his dinner companions to the waiters setting the table, is loaded with negative meaning to the Underground Man. We must keep in mind this tendency of the Underground Man to exaggerate or misinterpret events through his own bitterness and insecurity. Whenever he makes a judgment about a person or a place, we must take his skewed perspective into account.

Beyond providing us with further examples of how the Underground Man views other people, Chapter IV is also the first in the novel to give us a relatively clear picture of how others might view the Underground Man. Having been privy to his thoughts and feelings for a long time, we have begun to understand what motivates him. We can follow his logic to some degree, even if that logic is flawed. We are accustomed to his ways of looking at the world and at himself. We even begin to share his point of view. Since he worries so much about what other people think of him, we imagine that the other characters in the novel really do think about his behavior as much as he thinks they do. These other characters, however, have no understanding of the Underground Man's motives, and therefore his behavior appears bizarre to them. Their responses to his behavior are negative, but not necessarily because they are cruel or unfeeling people. For the most part, they are baffled by his rudeness.

The events of Chapter IV illustrate the Underground Man's masochism and indecisiveness. The fact that he remains at the dinner, pacing hopelessly in front of the other dinner guests but refusing to speak to them, indicates that he does indeed get a strange pleasure out of the feeling that he has hit rock bottom. As he has described in the "Underground" section, the Underground Man cultivates his own humiliation, almost deliberately hrowing himself into the most painful, inextricable situation imaginable. As he has also explained, he can never make decisive choices because he is always too conscious of every possibility. He thinks that if he allows himself to get deep enough into trouble, he will arrive at a point of inevitability. Once he reaches this point, it will be essential that he slap Zverkov's face. The Underground Man feels that at this point he might be able to find some kind of confidence or certainty.

Having reached a point of inevitability with his insulting speech to Zverkov, however, the Underground Man is still plagued by doubts. In Chapter V, he submits alternately to his romantic visions, his nihilistic realism, and his masochistic impulses. He imagines scenes of noble reconciliation with Zverkov, but he also realizes that these imagined scenes are ludicrous and have been lifted from literature. His visions of being beaten by everyone in the brothel are as much a masochistic fantasy as his visions of reconciliation are a Romantic one. At the same time, though, the Underground Man can understand the practical difficulties that dueling would present—for one thing, he does not have a single close friend to act as his second.

One of the major urges that drives the Underground Man to go to the brothel and confront Zverkov is the idea that he cannot avoid "life." He has attended the dinner partially to feel that he is living "life," and he believes that slapping Zverkov will be a "confrontation" with real life. The Underground Man seems to equate "life" with emotionally satisfying contact with other people—but the only emotions he can express are resentment, anger, and conflict. Believing that the underground protects him from life and therefore limits him, he feels that he can somehow escape his alienation through forced participation in life. In this light, his pursuit of Zverkov is genuinely a pursuit of freedom and dignity.

Chapter V also gives us a first glimpse at how the Underground Man directs his own self-loathing at others. Earlier in the novel, we see him resenting people who may have reason to disdain him or judge him. However, his timidity and indecision before these "active figures" have always prevented him from acting on his hatred. He has therefore always turned his anger or frustration on himself. In this chapter, we encounter people over whom the Underground Man can safely exert some power. The coachman and the prostitute are both members of the lower classes. Moreover, as the Underground Man is paying both of them for their services, he already exerts financial power over them. For someone like the Underground Man, who constantly feels impotent in his daily interactions with others, the ability to feel superior to another is somewhat intoxicating. With the coachman, the Underground Man can express his frustration with himself through physical violence—something he could never have done with the officer or Zverkov. Although the Underground Man is still somewhat intimidated by the young prostitute, wondering what she thinks of his appearance, he takes a certain pleasure in the fact that she will not enjoy her time with him but will not be able to do much about it.

PART II, CHAPTER VI–VII

SUMMARY: CHAPTER VI

The Underground Man wakes up after having slept with the young prostitute. He hears a clock wheezing, and he takes in the details of the dirty, narrow room where he has been sleeping. He remembers the events of the previous day as if they had happened a long time ago, and slowly he begins to feel anguished. Next to him, the prostitute opens her eyes and looks at him with indifferent curiosity. The Underground Man realizes that he has never spoken to her, and he suddenly feels disgusted with the idea of sex without any kind of love. They stare at each other, and the Underground Man becomes uncomfortable.

To break the silence, the Underground Man asks the prostitute's name, and she tells him that it is Liza. He continues to ask her about her background, but she seems unwilling to elaborate. Suddenly, he begins to tell her the story of a prostitute who died in a basement and whose former clients drank to her memory in a tavern. He then launches into a long, moralizing speech about the shamefulness of prostitution as a profession.

This lecture clearly moves Liza. The Underground Man becomes fascinated by the idea that he can elicit emotion in her. He feels that doing so indicates that he has some power over her. At the same time, he is genuinely interested in her, and feels emotionally unstable himself. He waxes sentimental about the value of family, describing the love he would feel for his daughter if he had one. When Liza implies that her own family may have sold her into prostitution, the Underground Man launches into a long speech about the value of marriage and the happiness it can bring. At the end of his speech, he tells Liza how much he loves little children, painting a glowing picture of a young mother and father with a plump, rosy baby. The Underground Man imagines that this picture will convince Liza to stop being a prostitute, but after he finishes his speech, he worries that she will laugh at him.

When Liza begins to speak, the Underground Man encourages her tenderly, but she tells him that his speech sounds like it was taken from a book. He is offended. In retrospect, he convinces himself that Liza's mockery was only a form of self-defense, and that she was genuinely moved by his speech. But at the moment he has not yet come to this revelation, and a "wicked feeling" comes over him.

SUMMARY: CHAPTER VII

The Underground Man defends himself against Liza's statement that his speech sounds like it was borrowed from a book. To the contrary, he says, the speech rose up in his soul in response to the baseness of Liza's situation. He feels vile for being with her because she is a prostitute. However, if she lived a purer life in a better place, he says, he might fall in love with her and accord her the respect that is denied a prostitute. He tries to convey to her how shameful and sordid her situation is. As a prostitute, she is throwing away her youth, her virtue, and her health. He continues his speech in brutal fashion, describing in detail Liza's inevitable death from consumption, predicting how ill-treated and friendless she will be in her illness, and how little respect she will get in death, as no one will mourn her.

The Underground Man gets so carried away in his speech that it takes him a while to realize that Liza is in complete despair, sobbing convulsively into her pillow. Suddenly horrified, he starts to get ready to leave. When he lights a candle, however, Liza gets up with a "half-crazed smile" and looks at him. He takes her hands and gives her his address, telling her to come to him. She promises to come, and he says goodbye to her.

Before the Underground Man can leave, however, Liza blushes and runs off to get something that she wants to show him. She returns joyfully with a love letter that she has received from a medical student whom she met at a dance. The student, who does not know she is a prostitute, professes his love in the letter with genuine emotion and respect. The Underground Man realizes that the letter is Liza's greatest treasure: she wants to show him that she has known honest, sincere love, and that she is not simply a degraded prostitute. The Underground Man leaves without saying anything, and walks home exhausted and perplexed. However, the "nasty truth" is starting to become clear.

ANALYSIS: CHAPTERS VI–VII

The Underground Man's speeches in these chapters provide another example of his inability to communicate—or to even conceive of any emotion other than bitterness—without using literature as a reference. Liza is quite right to say that the Underground Man's speech sounds as though it comes from a book. After his initial attempts to make casual conversation fail, the Underground Man falls back upon a popular nineteenth-century literary convention—the idea of the redeemed prostitute. Scenes in which a noble, almost fatherly male figure convinces a young, beautiful prostitute of the error of her ways abound in European writing. Indeed, the epigraph to "Apropos of the Wet Snow" is a selection from the Russian liberal poet Nikolai Nekrasov, written from the perspective of a man who has rescued a prostitute's "fallen soul" from "error's darkness" with "a word both sure and ardent." In the poem, the prostitute eventually becomes the man's wife. The scene in *Notes from Underground* draws much of its language and imagery from this tradition, and it is almost certainly a parody of a very similar scene in Chernyshevsky's novel *What Is to Be Done?*

Interestingly, the Underground Man does not, for once, recognize the literary tradition behind his mission. He feels that he is manipulating Liza with his sentimental language, and he both enjoys and feels ashamed of the feeling of power this manipulation gives him. He does not, however, appear to recognize the sources of his story as readily as he recognizes other literary influences to which he refers early in the novel. Instead, the Underground Man tells us in retrospect, he genuinely felt the things he was saying, even as he was aware that he was manipulating Liza. He feels for Liza and longs for genuine human contact, but his speech has little to do with his personal experience. He says that he loves children, but if so, he only loves them in theory. He has probably never witnessed a domestic scene like the one he describes, nor has he known anyone outside of novels in any kind of satisfying romantic relationship.

When the Underground Man describes the lonely life that he believes Liza will lead and her solitary death, he could be describing his own life. He has fewer friends than Liza does, and we sense that it is likely no one will ever mourn his death, not even in a tavern over a few beers. It is telling, too, that his initial description of the prostitute's death involves a coffin being removed from a basement. A more accurate translation for the title of *Notes from Underground* might be "Memoirs from a Cellar."

The Underground Man may not be consciously aware of the similarities between the marginalized life of a prostitute and his own alienation from the world, but these similarities may account for his intense desire to prove that he is morally and intellectually superior to Liza. However, the greatest difference between them is that the Underground Man, however much he occasionally waxes sentimental, cannot cope with displays of genuine emotion. As he has suggested before, he has little or no experience with "real life," and his confrontations with it send him running back to the underground for safety. After delivering his long and impassioned speech, delighted that his words seemed to be affecting Liza, the Underground Man is horrified by her passionate sobbing. He has some contempt for Liza's love letter, yet he pities her for the fact that she feels she needs to prove to him that she is worthy of noble love. The Underground Man's contempt could easily be read as jealousy—there is no one to love him, and he has no treasured tokens to prove that he is lovable at all.

Part II, Chapter VIII

Summary

The next day, the Underground Man is horrified by his "sentimental" behavior with Liza, and especially by the fact that he gave her his address. He is more immediately concerned, though, with how he can redeem himself in the eyes of Zverkov and Simonov. The Underground Man borrows money from Anton Antonych to pay his debt to Simonov, casually explaining that he had been "carousing" with friends the night before. Then he writes a letter of apology to Simonov, carefully cultivating a "gentlemanly, good-natured" tone. The Underground Man boastfully exults in his ability to use his education and intelligence to get out of an awkward situation, and he almost convinces himself that he does indeed view the events of the night before as casually as he seems to in the letter.

The Underground Man then takes a walk in the crowded streets, but he begins to feel more and more confused and guilty. He worries that Liza will really visit him, and he fears that she will be unimpressed by his shabby apartment, his rude servant, and his own attempts at courtesy. He remembers his behavior with her as dishonorable, but then tells himself that he really did want to inspire noble thoughts in her.

After Liza does not come that evening, he spends a few days both dreading and anticipating her arrival. Certain that she will find him, the Underground Man curses her "pure heart" and "rotten sentimental soul," but he also constructs elaborate fantasies in which he saves her from prostitution, educates her, and compels her to fall in love with him. In these fantasies, he is too unselfish and refined to accept her love initially, but in the end, he invites her into his life with the last lines of the poem quoted at the beginning of Part II: "and now, full mistress of the place, / Come bold and free into my house." These fantasies, predictably, end in self-disgust.

The Underground Man is distracted from his frustrations by the rudeness of his elderly servant, Apollon. He hates Apollon because he believes that Apollon is vain and pedantic. He feels that Apollon looks down on him, condescending to allow the Underground Man to pay him seven roubles a month to "do nothing." The Underground Man especially hates Apollon's cultivated lisp, thinking that Apollon is unjustifiably proud of his distinguished way of speaking. However, the Underground Man feels that he cannot afford to get rid of Apollon, because he imagines that it would be impossible to separate Apollon from the apartment.

Although the Underground Man concludes that he has no control over Apollon, he attempts to exert some power by intentionally withholding Apollon's wages for two weeks. He hopes to force Apollon into swallowing his pride and lowering himself to ask for his wages, rather than of proudly waiting for them to be delivered. Unfortunately, every time the Underground Man attempts this trick, Apollon's significant sighs and stares defeat him. Unable to meet Apollon's gaze, the Underground Man always caves in and gives him the money. On this occasion, however, the Underground Man explodes with intense anger after one of Apollon's long, significant looks. He threatens and insults Apollon, showing him the wage money but refusing to give it to him. Apollon threatens to go to the police.

The Underground Man decides that Liza is responsible for the problem he is having with Apollon. Just as the Underground Man is about to hit Apollon, Liza enters the room unannounced. The Underground Man is overcome by shame when he sees her. He flees to his bedroom until Apollon comes to tell him that "someone" has come to see him.

Analysis

The Underground Man's cheerfulness the morning after he writes the letter to Simonov indicates the degree to which he has learned to delude himself about the realities of life. Convinced of his own virtues as a letter-writer, the Underground Man believes he has set everything right with his friend. This complacency not only demonstrates the Underground Man's egotism, but also shows how the he finds ways to cope with frequent humiliation.

In characteristic fashion, the Underground Man alternates between looking forward to Liza's visit and dreading the fact that she will see the shabbiness of his apartment. As we have seen, the Underground Man has an extraordinarily delicate ego, alternately exulting in his own intelligence and then plunging into shame. This tendency, combined with the fact that the Underground Man has never had a mutually respectful and pleasant relationship with anyone, supports the opinion the Underground Man has already expressed about love—that love means dominating someone until they have totally submitted. When the Underground Man considers his relationship with Liza, he feels that either he or she inevitably will have to be humiliated. Though he feels confident about his dominant role as the prostitute-rescuer at a brothel, he feels vulnerable to judgment and derision in his own apartment.

The Underground Man's burning hatred of Apollon stems from a similar desire for domination. The Underground Man wants to feel he can dominate Apollon completely, as Apollon is his servant and depends on him for wages. The Underground Man's attempts to make Apollon submit to his will are no more successful than his attempt to bump into the officer in the park. The Underground Man perhaps attributes some of his own strange pride to Apollon, just as some of his hatred of Apollon perhaps comes from his hatred of anyone he imagines is able to look down on him.

Part II, Chapter IX

Summary

> *[S]he was going to pay dearly for it all . . .*
>
> (See QUOTATIONS, p. 61)

The Underground Man feels humiliated because Liza has seen his ratty bathrobe and witnessed his behavior toward Apollon. He orders the embarrassed Liza to sit down, and then makes a confused attempt to explain the situation, secretly thinking that he will make Liza pay for making him feel so humiliated. He gives Apollon his wages and sends him to buy tea. After a haughty Apollon has left the apartment, the Underground Man launches into a violent tirade against him, alarming Liza as he bursts into tears. Even in the middle of his tantrum, though, the Underground Man is conscious of "putting on a show," and he feels ashamed. He blames Liza for his embarrassment and becomes extremely resentful toward her, imagining he could kill her. He decides to stop talking in order to punish her, and he remains silent even when Liza timidly ventures that she wants to leave the brothel forever.

When Liza gets up to leave, thinking she has disturbed the Underground Man, he suddenly explodes in a long, disorganized speech. He tells Liza that he never intended to save her from prostitution. Instead, he manipulated her with "pathetic words" so that he could humiliate her as Zverkov and the others had humiliated him earlier that night at dinner. The Underground Man tells Liza that he was only interested in exerting power over her, but that in a moment of weakness and fear he gave her his address. He adds that his greatest worry over the last three days has been that she might see him in his shabby dressing gown, and that she might learn that he is not the great hero she may have believed him to be. Now he will never forgive her for seeing him in this sordid environment, nor will he forgive her for listening to his hysterical speech.

At the beginning of the tirade, Liza is crushed, but by the end she understands that the Underground Man is unhappy, and she is filled with an agonizing sympathy for him. She throws her arms around him and begins to cry. The Underground Man responds by throwing himself face down on the sofa and sobbing for fifteen minutes.

Soon, the Underground Man begins to feel ashamed again, realizing that the roles have been reversed: in the brothel it was Liza who lay face down and sobbed while the Underground Man preached to her, but now Liza is the heroine and the Underground Man is the "humiliated creature." When he gets up from the sofa, he wants to dominate Liza again. She misreads his hatred and desire for revenge as genuine passion, and embraces him.

Analysis

At the beginning of Chapter IX, the Underground Man notes that he will make Liza "pay dearly" for "this." We might ask ourselves what "this" is: his shameful house, his clothes, his nervous demeanor, his ugly face, or perhaps his miserable future. Liza becomes the repository for all the aggression he has built up against those he perceives as having slighted him throughout life. In this way, the Underground Man makes a transition from victim to victimizer. When Liza responds to the Underground Man's tirade with sympathy and affection rather than horror or anger, we understand for the first time that she is a truly sensitive, perceptive, and loving person. She is intuitive enough to see that the Underground Man's cruel words stem from his insecurity, loneliness, and pride. Because she is grateful to the Underground Man for opening her eyes to the futility of her own situation as a prostitute, she naturally wants to help him as he has helped her. Even if she had not been grateful to the Underground Man, she might have responded in the same way, out of a human instinct to comfort anyone who is suffering.

This revelation of Liza's true character is somewhat ironic in the context of the novel. Throughout Part II, we have seen the Underground Man try to make the world around him fit the conventions of Romantic literature; now we see how the real world thwarts his attempts. Officers are never honorable, duels are never fought, and no one appreciates the Underground Man's sensitivity or his esteem for "the beautiful and lofty" as much as they should. We might expect the Underground Man's attempt to impose another literary convention—the redeemed prostitute—upon the banal realities of 1840s St. Petersburg to end in total failure. Based on what we have seen in the novel thus far, we expect the prostitute to laugh at the Underground Man's impassioned speeches just as the officer would have laughed at the idea of a duel. At the very least, we expect the prostitute to turn out to be as coarse and narrow-minded as all the people the Underground Man derides. Instead, Liza is a heroine worthy of a Romantic novel—gentle, simple, and kind.

Unfortunately, because the Underground Man has never been the object of this kind of interest and sympathy, he has no idea how to handle it. When Liza first puts her arms around the Underground Man, he is so confused that he bursts into tears and allows her to comfort him. It must come as an immense relief for him to receive love and tenderness after a lifetime of indifference and abuse. In this light, the Underground Man's reaction is entirely understandable, as he is finally given an opportunity to display an emotion other than anger or resentment. However, we remember the Underground Man's comments in Part I about the intense shame he feels after displays of "sentimentality" or emotion. We also remember that the only way he can think of love is as a sadomasochistic relationship in which one person dominates and the other is dominated. Rather than concentrate on love as a mutual exchange of tenderness and sympathy, in which he and Liza might comfort each other, the Underground Man can only see that the roles in their relationship have been reversed. He has lost his power over Liza, and now she dominates him. Liza is the only person in the novel over whom the Underground Man has felt any true sense of power, and he is furious with her for taking that power away from him. His sentiment toward her quickly turns to hate, as he wants to reclaim his power over her and wants to punish her for taking this power away from him. At the end of the chapter, the Underground Man resolves to exert his power over Liza physically, by possessing her sexually and treating her as a prostitute even as she believes they are engaging in an act of love.

Part II, Chapter X

Summary

As the final chapter opens, the Underground Man is running frantically around his room and looking at Liza through a crack between the screens in the wall. Liza realizes that the Underground Man's desire for her does not come from love, but from a desire to humiliate and dominate her. She realizes that he hates her and envies her.

The Underground Man explains why he is incapable of love. He says that, for him, love consists only of the right to tyrannize someone else. He cannot understand unselfish love, and he has failed to understand that Liza has come to see him because of love rather than because of his elaborate, "pathetic" speeches. At this point, though, the Underground Man only wants "peace"—the pressure of "living life" and interacting with others is becoming too much for him.

Liza gets up to leave. The Underground Man forces some money into her hand in a last, malicious attempt to humiliate her. He claims in his narration that the urge to humiliate her did not come from his heart; he did it only because it seemed appropriately literary, and after he did it he was ashamed.

The Underground Man calls after Liza immediately after she leaves, but she does not respond. He hears the door slam as she leaves the building. A minute later, he finds the money he gave her crumpled on the table, realizing that she threw it away before she left the apartment. The Underground Man is shocked that Liza could be capable of such a noble action. He runs after her into the falling snow, but she is gone. The Underground Man is distraught and wants to beg her forgiveness. He declares that he will never remember this moment with indifference. A moment later, though, he convinces himself that Liza will be purified and elevated by the hatred and forgiveness that his insult will inspire in her. At the same time, he is conscious of the literary merit of his own thoughts, and feels ashamed that he is focusing on that literary merit rather than on Liza's welfare.

Back in the present, the flashback finished, the Underground Man decides that "all this comes out somehow none too well in my recollection." He decides that perhaps he will end his notes at this point. He wonders if he should have written them at all, for they are not "literature, but corrective punishment." His antisocial life in the underground is "not interesting," especially since he is not a hero, but rather an antihero whose dread of "living life" is all too familiar to the reader. The Underground Man accuses his readers of having all of the problems that he has, but refusing to carry them through to their logical conclusion. Perhaps, he suggests, he is more "living" than his more active readers.

Suggesting that modern men, ashamed of the fleshly reality of their lives, retreat more and more into abstract ideas, the Underground Man decides not to write any more notes. A note Dostoevsky writes at the end tells us that the Underground Man could not keep this resolution to stop writing, and instead continued to write compulsively. Dostoevsky writes that this point in the notes seems like a good place to stop, however, so the novel ends here.

Analysis

Many critics consider the moment when Liza slams the door to be the climax of the second half of *Notes from Underground*. Liza is perhaps the only hope for the Underground Man's redemption, as she is perceptive and patient enough to see through his proud, hostile façade to understand his mental anguish. In short, she is kind enough to care about him. In this last chapter, when Liza casts away the money, we—and the Underground Man—understand that she is also noble, moral, and as proud as the Underground Man himself.

The discovery of the crumpled bill is an important moment for the Underground Man. His self-absorption and lack of positive experiences with others have not prepared him for the possibility that other people could perform noble gestures such as Liza's. She has a genuine sense of the "beautiful and lofty" herself, though it is couched in modesty, shyness, and simplicity. Liza could have emerged from the pages of any sentimental novel or poem. Somehow, the Underground Man's artificial pastiche of literary conventions in the brothel has found him a real-life romantic heroine. The slamming door, however, signals Liza's irrevocable disappearance from his life, and its sound resounds throughout the building. The Underground Man has been shut underground for good, with no more chances of escape.

When Liza has gone, the Underground Man immediately begins to rationalize her departure. Unsurprisingly, although he is totally unable to handle the responsibility of a relationship with her while she is present, in retrospect he imagines that he has been an important event in her life. He believes that the initial hatred and eventual forgiveness she will feel toward him will purify and elevate her. In reality, Liza could perhaps have purified and elevated the Underground Man, but he cannot allow himself to recognize the regret he feels. Even though he declares that he will never recall the moment with indifference, we see that he has already begun to try to lessen its emotional importance. When he focuses on the literary merits of his thoughts about Liza, he reproaches himself for his egoism—but that very egoism is the only tool he has to distract himself from the significance of Liza's departure. The Underground Man's distrust of his own emotional responses comes partially from his general skepticism about the good of human beings. This distrust also allows him to endure his existence underground: if he believes that his emotions are artificial, then he can discount them.

The Underground Man's statement that he will "never . . . recall this moment with indifference" is also important to the structure of *Notes from Underground.* Some commentators have found the novel's two-part structure strange, as the second part comes chronologically before the first. We have already seen how this structure works to illuminate and explain the Underground Man's character, using concrete examples from the second part to illustrate abstract statements from the first part. This quotation from the end of the second part unifies the two "fragments," as the twenty-four-year-old Underground Man seems to be speaking almost directly to the forty-year-old Underground Man who is narrating his story. By the end of the novel, we see that the Underground Man is still unable to recall the moment of Liza's departure with indifference. We understand why he has chosen this particular memory for his strange memoir: it is the moment at which it becomes certain that the twenty-four-year-old Underground Man will become the forty-year-old Underground Man, totally isolated and alienated in his "underground." We also understand why he feels that it is time to end his notes for good. He has lived through a crucial moment in his life, and he feels no better for having lived through it. He only recognizes the significance of his loss.

The Underground Man ends his notes with an accusation aimed at us, his audience. He tells us that we are all like him in a way, but that we lack the courage to take our lives to the extreme to which he has taken his. We probably do not want to believe this statement, and we certainly would not consider ourselves better off if we lived the same life as the Underground Man. Dostoevsky, however, is using the Underground Man to show us how modern urban life does alienate us from ourselves and other people. Most contemporary readers of *Notes from Underground* refused to recognize themselves in the Underground Man. They preferred to consider him an interesting psychological study of a highly abnormal person rather than a casualty of societal problems to which they, too, were exposed. However, the Underground Man's theories and behavior resonate in much of modern literature, from Dostoevsky's later novels to Jean-Paul Sartre, Albert Camus, and others. As the western world has absorbed *Notes from Underground* into its cultural heritage, its literature seems to have decided that there are many more people living underground than we might have guessed.

Important Quotations Explained

1. "Ha, ha, ha! Next you'll be finding pleasure in a toothache!" you will exclaim, laughing.

   "And why not? There is also pleasure in a toothache," I will answer.

This passage, which begins Chapter IV of the "Underground" section, illustrates the extent of the Underground Man's masochism. In the previous chapter, he has described in great detail the ways in which he takes pleasure in his own humiliation, enjoying the extremity of his indecision and powerlessness. The "you" in the quotation is the Underground Man's imagined audience, to which the entire novel is addressed. This audience represents the perspective of the rational man, who would certainly scoff at the perverse idea that someone could enjoy something that brings him pain. The statement that the Underground Man will next be finding pleasure in a toothache is sarcastic, a dismissal of the absurdity of the situation. No one in their right mind could take pleasure in a toothache.

Always ready to take an idea to its extreme, and eager to disprove any unshakable assumptions his audience might have about reason and nature, the Underground Man brings the perversity of his idea to the next level: there is indeed pleasure in a toothache. He goes on to describe the aesthetic value of the moans of someone suffering from a toothache. His moans are "conscious" moans, the moans of a "developed" man who has been exposed to European civilization and understands that true art has no purpose besides itself. The developed man will construct elaborate, symphonic moans and groans that will give him the satisfaction of irritating his friends and family.

The reference to European civilization relates the idea of the toothache to the question of the value of European culture's influence on Russia. Indeed, the Underground Man's pleasure in his toothache is an indication not only of his masochism and his desire to perplex his audience, but of the artificiality of his existence. His enjoyment of the toothache becomes a parody of his enjoyment of other "developed" pleasures, encouraged by European literature and philosophy. Dostoevsky was extremely critical of the way in which this Europeanized, "developed" way of thinking alienated Russian intellectuals from the real culture and people of Russia, who worked with the soil as members of a community. The refinements that the Underground Man exaggerates in this passage are both a result of and a contributing factor to his isolation from society.

2. Oh, gentlemen, perhaps I really regard myself as an intelligent man only because throughout my entire life I've never been able to start or finish anything.

The Underground Man makes this statement in Chapter V of "Underground," after having described the causes and conditions of his inertia. Just prior to this point in the novel, he has asserted that his intelligence is the cause of his inertia; now he suggests that his inertia is evidence of his intelligence. This reversal demonstrates the Underground Man's belief that intelligence, or consciousness, must cause inertia and indecision in the modern era. According to the Underground Man, a man must be completely confident that he is doing the right thing before he can take action. He needs a "primary" cause, something solid by which he can justify what he does. A stupid man can imagine that he has found a primary cause, but an intelligent man knows that this primary cause is really a secondary cause, which is related to all kinds of different concepts and problems that would take an eternity to sort out. A narrow-minded man thinks that the reason he wants revenge on someone else is for the sake of justice; an intelligent man is aware that he is not motivated by justice at all. The intelligent man fails to find a satisfactory reason for the action he wants to perform, and, in fact, is impossible to find one. For the intelligent man, even the laws of nature and reason are suspect. Therefore, no intelligent man should ever be able to make up his mind to start or finish anything—no matter how simple. The intelligent man will constantly be aware that he has no concrete reason to take action, or will at least be aware that he has no understanding of the reason to take action.

3. Who wants to want according to a little table?

The Underground Man asks this question of his imagined audience in Chapter VIII of "Underground," after his audience has explained to him that his argument about the primacy of the human will is flawed. His audience has brought up the idea that scientific rules and formulas can explain the origins of and reasons for human desires. By this argument, if there is a scientific formula for human happiness, that same formula would also explain man's desire to exercise free will, and would explain the reason for the existence of free will in the first place. Therefore, it is absurd to assert that a scientific formula for human happiness limits the rights of man to exercise free will. The Underground Man's response to this argument is paradoxical. If science can explain why human beings desire anything, it can certainly explain why human beings would or would not desire "to want according to a little table." The Underground Man's assertion, however, is incontestable. No matter how much science manages to explain about the nature of human desires, it cannot change the fact that those desires exist. Furthermore, no matter how strong the evidence that human beings do "want according to a little table"—that is, according to a set of rational, predictable formulas—most humans treasure the idea that their desires are independent and unique. Hence, they would not appreciate the idea that their desires are completely predictable. The contrast between the image of a tiny, well-regulated, boring little multiplication table and the great urgency and power of the word "want" is very effective in proving the Underground Man's point. No matter how the numbers add up, describing human desires in terms of a "little table" seems like the worst kind of oversimplification, and makes even the most sensible people want to rebel against reason and go running headlong into a stone wall.

4. Here it is, here it is at last, the encounter with reality. . . . All is lost now!

The Underground Man says these words to himself at the beginning of Chapter V of "Apropos of the Wet Snow," as he is running down the stairs in pursuit of his former schoolmates. The others have left Zverkov's farewell dinner—at which the Underground Man has utterly humiliated himself and alienated them—to go to a brothel together. The Underground Man has resolved to follow them, either to receive an apology or to exact his revenge. He is elated for a number of reasons. For one, he feels that his strange brand of masochism has finally brought him to the lowest possible position, and being in this position has made some kind of confrontation inevitable. For someone as indecisive as the Underground Man, the thought of inevitability is reassuring. He is certain that the situation will resolve itself in some way, ending in either triumph or defeat. Either end will involve an "encounter with reality": the Underground Man will finally be forced to participate in "life," to interact with other human beings in a meaningful way. The Underground Man craves this kind of interaction, and every time he is faced with "some external event, no matter how small," he thinks it is going to break the monotonous, lonely pattern of his life. This event promises to be monumental: a duel, or a fistfight, or the adoring and apologetic friendship of a former enemy. It is telling that the Underground Man should think of this "encounter with reality" in terms of violence. Anger, revenge, and bitterness seem to be the only realistic ways in which he can conceive of interacting with others. Consequently, he imagines duels and arguments as the only way he can participate in the social world. The Underground Man's association of reality with violence and anger, pride and humiliation, foreshadows the failure of his relationship with Liza. He has no tools for friendship that do not involve aggression.

5. I sensed vaguely that she was going to pay dearly *for it all. . . .*

In this quotation, from Chapter IX of "Apropos of the Wet Snow," the Underground Man remembers his reaction to Liza's arrival at his apartment. He has been shrieking with rage at his servant, Apollon, and is dressed in a ragged bathrobe. When Liza enters the apartment, the Underground Man "die[s] of shame" and runs into his room in a panic. When he returns, he tries to appear dignified, but continues to feel extreme embarrassment. He is infuriated by Liza's patient, expectant stare, as he feels pressure to do something impressive to equal his speech in the brothel. The Underground Man's humiliation is increased by the fact that in the brothel, when he was convincing Liza of the error of her ways, he felt enormous power over her. He felt he could manipulate her emotions, influence her choices about her own life, and control how she felt about herself and about him. He imagined that she admired and respected him. These feelings were particularly valuable to the Underground Man after his humiliation at Zverkov's farewell dinner. Now he has lost his temper in front of Apollon, the one person over whom he feels he should have some control. The Underground Man therefore feels particularly powerless, imagining he has lost all respect and dignity in Liza's eyes. He holds her responsible for the fact that she has seen him in this miserable situation. Her presence has made him aware of the shabbiness of his bathroom, his apartment, his behavior with Apollon—the shabbiness of his entire existence. In this way, the Underground Man transfers the responsibility for all of his unhappiness to Liza's shoulders. Just as he can turn his hatred of others toward himself, he can turn his hatred of himself toward others, especially when they are weaker, poorer, and of less respectable than he.

Key Facts

FULL TITLE
Notes from Underground or *Zapiski iz podpol'ya*

AUTHOR
Fyodor Dostoevsky

TYPE OF WORK
Novel

GENRE
Satire; social critique; fictional memoir; existential novel; psychological study

LANGUAGE
Russian

TIME AND PLACE WRITTEN
1863; St. Petersburg

DATE OF FIRST PUBLICATION
January–April 1864

PUBLISHER
Epoch magazine

NARRATOR
The anonymous narrator of *Notes from Underground* is also the novel's protagonist. The Underground Man is a bitter, reclusive forty-year-old civil servant speaking from his St. Petersburg apartment in the 1860s, though he spends the second section of the novel describing his life as a younger man in the 1840s.

POINT OF VIEW
The narrator speaks in the first person, describing his own thoughts and feelings and narrating events that occurred sixteen years earlier in his life.

TONE
The Underground Man is a prime example of an unreliable narrator. Because the whole novel is told through his skewed and irrational perspective, we cannot take his depictions of

events and characters at face value. We also cannot assume that the Underground Man's perspective is the same as Dostoevsky's. The author maintains a considerable distance between his view and the narrator's. Often, we see Dostoevsky satirizing an event that the Underground Man sees as very serious.

TENSE

The first section of the novel is told in the present tense. In the second half, the Underground Man narrates a long story from his past, telling this story in past tense with occasional present-tense commentary.

SETTING (TIME)

Approximately 1863 in "Underground" and 1847 in "Apropos of the Wet Snow"

SETTING (PLACE)

St. Petersburg

PROTAGONIST

The protagonist is the same as the narrator, the Underground Man.

MAJOR CONFLICT

The Underground Man rejects many of the values and assumptions of the society in which he lives, and this conflict often manifests itself in smaller, resentful conflicts between the Underground Man and other people who represent the problems he has with society.

RISING ACTION

The Underground Man's various attempts to interact with society, including his attempt to fight a duel, his bungled dinner with four of his school acquaintances, and his attempts to rescue a prostitute, Liza, from her life of sin

CLIMAX

Liza's positive response to the Underground Man, quickly followed by his cruel and resentful rejection of her because of his inexperience with love and kindness; Liza's departure, signifying the loss of the Underground Man's last chance to escape the underground with her

FALLING ACTION
The Underground Man's increased distancing of himself from society and further slinking into the "underground"; his resignation from his civil service job; his self-imposed isolation in his apartment; his abandonment of his youthful idealism and his desires to participate in the social world

THEMES
The fallacies of rationalism and utopianism; the artificiality of Russian culture; the paralysis of the conscious man in modern society

MOTIFS
The wet snow; *l'homme de la nature et de la vérité*; the redeemed prostitute

SYMBOLS
The underground; St. Petersburg; the Crystal Palace; money

FORESHADOWING
The Underground Man's declaration that his idea of love is the total domination of another person foreshadows his inability to forge a relationship with Liza. The Underground Man's mention of a vague desire to make Liza pay for seeing him in a humiliating situation foreshadows his later attempts to humiliate her. (In a sense, the entire first section of the novel foreshadows the second by giving us tools to understand the Underground Man's behavior. However, the first section does not hint at the events of the second section specifically enough to be considered true foreshadowing.)

Study Questions & Essay Topics

Study Questions

1. *How much should we trust what the Underground Man tells us? Pick one section of the text in which you feel he is particularly reliable or unreliable, and discuss what this might tell us about the text as a whole.*

Though there are many passages in the novel to consider in this context, an especially appropriate one might be the Underground Man's description of his servant Apollon in Chapter XIII of "Apropos of the Wet Snow." In this passage, the Underground Man describes Apollon as pedantic, vain, and extremely disdainful of the Underground Man. He complains that when Apollon does any work at all, he completes it "as if he were bestowing the highest favor upon me." Apollon comes off as a truly insufferable person, and initially we sympathize with the Underground Man for having to put up with him.

A closer analysis of the Underground Man's description, however, reveals that most of his complaints against Apollon regard his servant's physical description. The Underground Man is annoyed with the way Apollon styles his hair, with the expression on his face, and with his lisp, even though the Underground Man admits Apollon only lisps because "his tongue was a bit longer than it should have been." If we look through the text for any evidence of Apollon actually exhibiting rude behavior, we find that though he does speak somewhat haughtily to the Underground Man, he does so only after the Underground Man has hurled unprovoked insults and abuse at him. We must also consider that an important component of what we know about the Underground Man comes from his interactions with other people. For instance, in the dinner scene, when we see the Underground Man explode at Zverkov in the same way he explodes at Apollon, the other characters' reactions help us to understand how irrational the Underground Man's behavior appears. In the scene with Apollon, however, we have access only to the Under-

QUESTIONS & ESSAYS

ground Man's account of the conflict. We know that the Underground Man's pride has been hurt, that he is anxious about Liza's possible arrival, that he is ashamed of his apartment and his servant, that he is feeling powerless, and that he has a tendency to take his aggression out on other people. Knowing what we do and lacking any real evidence of Apollon's allegedly rude behavior, we can infer that the Underground Man's narration is unreliable here. Throughout the novel, then, we must keep in mind that we cannot always trust the Underground Man's descriptions of other characters whose perspectives we do not get to hear.

2. *The Underground Man uses several images or phrases—the Golden Age, the idea of the crystal palace, "two times-two-makes-four," the mouse-man, and so on—as metaphors to convey his ideas. Pick two of these images and discuss their relationship with each other and with the Underground Man's arguments.*

The crystal palace and the idea of "two-times-two-makes-four" are both related to the Underground Man's argument against mankind's excessive trust in reason. Both are metaphors for the tendency of progressive thinkers and "rational egoists" to set up "laws of reason" as absolutes beyond all possible doubt. The crystal palace symbolizes the ideal utopian society that humanity will be able to achieve once it has discovered all of the laws of nature that govern human behavior. "Two-times-two-makes-four" represents all mathematical laws which have been proved inalienably true. The application of laws such as these is what will make the crystal palace possible. The Underground Man distrusts these laws because, though they might work in logical formulas, he does not think they can be applied to human beings. He believes that to shut up humanity in a crystal palace based on the law of "two-times-two-makes-four" destroys the complexity and variety of human personalities. Such overly rigid thinking discounts the importance of individual free will, which the Underground Man claims will always want to run up against the "stone wall" of logical fact. It is impossible to disprove "two-times-two-equals-four," and since the crystal palace is built on "two-times-two-equals-four," it follows that it is impossible to protest the crystal palace. By definition, the crystal palace is good for humankind. But the Underground Man wants to be able to stick his tongue out at the crystal palace, and he says that "two-times-two-equals-five" is sometimes more satisfying than "two-times-two-equals-four." The human mind delights in the irrational as much as the rational, which implies that the human experience includes, but is not limited to "two-times-two-equals-four," and therefore cannot be confined to the crystal palace.

3. *Much of the Underground Man's social world centers on people whom he integrates into his power structure. How does this obsession with rank and power manifest itself throughout* Notes from Underground*? How it is consistent with the Underground Man's character?*

Whenever the Underground Man meets another person, he immediately feels the need to size him or her up in comparison to himself. He usually decides that he is much more intelligent, conscious, and sensitive than the other person, but he is nonetheless almost always intimidated by the person's confidence, wealth, attractiveness, or social standing. The Underground Man feels a strange mixture of smug pride—stemming from his knowledge of his superior intellect—and such deep shame about his clothes, his job, his face, or his apartment that he cannot bear to look the other person in the face. His shame before others makes him resent them even more, until he strongly desires to hurt or humiliate them as punishment for making him feel this shame. However, because the Underground Man feels so inferior to them, he is powerless to do anything about these desires. As a result, he is obsessed with power relationships. He craves the attention of the people whom he believes to have power over him, like the officer and his former schoolmates, while believing he should be able to exert power over them at the same time. Because the Underground Man's constant feeling of powerlessness is painful to him, he seeks out situations in which he can feel powerful. He wants to dominate those whom he feels he outranks in social or economic standing, such his servant, Apollon, or the prostitute Liza. However, the Underground Man's obsession with maintaining his power over others is so strong that any normal reversal of power in the relationship—Apollon expecting his wages, Liza seeing the Underground Man in a position of distress or embarrassment—fills him with shame and rage. Having accepted the superiority of people he sees as higher in rank than he, he expects to be able to feel the same kind of superiority over those who are lower than he. Any disturbance of that power structure is damaging to his ego.

Suggested Essay Topics

1. Some critics see the Underground Man as insane, while others see him as a fairly lucid—if maladjusted—observer of society and his place within it. Evaluate the Underground Man's sanity, using concrete examples from the text.

2. The city of St. Petersburg is an important presence throughout the novel. Select one passage and explain how St. Petersburg affects the Underground Man. How does the city function as a character in the text?

3. Though the Underground Man is not meant to represent Dostoevsky himself, interesting comparisons can be drawn between the two. What are the most significant similarities and differences between them?

4. Dostoevsky was famously wary of the Roman Catholic church. What evidence for this bias can be found in Part I of *Notes from Underground*?

5. Dostoevsky had a great talent for showing his readers the world through the confused eyes of his characters. How does he use this ability to heighten, rather than diminish, the sense of realism in the novel?

6. Though elements of *Notes from Underground* are tragic, the text is not a "tragedy" in the formal sense. How does Dostoevsky create this modern, realist story in a manner very different from the classical literary expectations of tragedy? Which elements from older forms of tragedy does he include, and which does he exclude?

7. The Underground Man abhors the way in which progressive thinkers of his era worship reason, but he does not necessarily totally reject reason outright. Discuss his attitude toward reason and logic. What value does he assign to logical, rational thinking, and how does he make use of it? For a starting point, pick a passage and begin your discussion with a close reading.

Review & Resources

Quiz

1. Why would the Underground Man be pleased if people called him a "lazybones"?

    A. People would think he was rich and did not have to work for a living
    B. It would be something by which to define himself
    C. "Lazybones" is a Russian slang term for someone who is successful with women
    D. He thinks he gets too much credit for the work he does in his department

2. When does the Underground Man visit Anton Antonych at home?

    A. When he needs to have a tooth pulled
    B. When he wants to borrow money
    C. Every Thursday morning
    D. When he has the urge to socialize, if it happens to be a Tuesday

3. How does the Underground Man prepare for his confrontation with the officer in the park?

    A. He takes boxing lessons
    B. He buys a pair of gloves and a beaver collar
    C. He bribes a park attendant to trip the officer
    D. He compiles a list of witty retorts to use in case the officer insults him

4. When do the other guests arrive at Zverkov's dinner?

    A. At the same time that the Underground Man arrives
    B. Before the Underground Man arrives
    C. After the Underground Man arrives
    D. They never arrive

5. What does Liza show the Underground Man before he leaves the brothel?

   A. A picture of herself as a little girl
   B. A list of the St. Petersburg luminaries she has bedded
   C. A love letter from a medical student
   D. A bracelet that her mother gave her before she died

6. What does the Underground Man think of the theory that, as civilization progresses, mankind becomes less likely to wage war?

   A. He agrees, because he thinks that developed men of the nineteenth century are too indecisive to take any action at all, least of all starting or fighting a war
   B. He disagrees, because he thinks that war gives the individual a chance to show his valor and ingenuity and achieve glory and heroism
   C. He agrees, because he thinks that civilization's emphasis on reason will cause all disputes to be resolved by contests of intellect rather than force
   D. He disagrees, because the amount of war and bloodshed in the nineteenth century surpasses the amount of war and bloodshed in previous, less civilized eras

7. Why does the Underground Man decide not to give Apollon his wages?

   A. He wants to show that he has the ability to exert power over Apollon
   B. Apollon forgot to shine the Underground Man's boots
   C. He has spent the money he was saving for Apollon's wages, so he has no more money left
   D. He has decided to give Apollon a present instead

8. When the Underground Man was in school, how did he earn some respect from his fellow students?

   A. He seduced the headmaster's daughter
   B. He wrote beautiful stories that moved them to tears
   C. He had great academic success
   D. He bested Zverkov in a duel

9. For what does the Underground Man say he will make Liza "pay dearly"?

   A. For seeing him in an embarrassing situation
   B. For sleeping with Zverkov
   C. For stealing money from him
   D. For rejecting his advances

10. Why does the Underground Man call the second half of his memoir "Apropos of the Wet Snow"?

   A. He is quoting a Pushkin poem of the same title
   B. He is implying that the snow is wet with his tears
   C. Because the falling snow reminds him of another day when snow was falling
   D. Because winter is his favorite season

11. Why does the Underground Man dislike the idea of the Crystal Palace?

   A. It represents the ruling classes' oppression of the serfs
   B. He believes that using crystal for architecture is a waste of money
   C. He would not be able to stick out his tongue at it
   D. He would not want to live in a palace with transparent walls

12. What does the Underground Man put in Liza's hand before she leaves his apartment?

   A. Money
   B. A letter
   C. A book
   D. A ring

13. How does the Underground Man make amends for his behavior at Zverkov's farewell dinner?

   A. He invites the men out for drinks at his expense
   B. He writes an apology to Simonov and pays him back the money he owes
   C. He writes an article in praise of Zverkov in the paper
   D. He pays for the men to visit prostitutes

14. Why did the Underground Man's one close friendship fall apart?

    A. He borrowed his friend's money and could not repay
    B. The friend wore lemon-colored gloves, which the Underground Man thought were in poor taste
    C. He demanded that his friend totally submit to his will, and then hated the friend once he had submitted
    D. The friend grew exasperated with the Underground Man's belligerence and threw him out a window

15. Why does the Underground Man think that active men stop pursuing their goals once they hit a wall?

    A. They are too stupid to think of a way around the wall
    B. They have confidence in facts, and it is a fact that one cannot go through a wall
    C. Something near the wall distracts them
    D. They run into the wall and end up in the hospital

16. Why does the Underground Man sleep with Liza at his apartment?

    A. He wants to prove that he loves her
    B. He wants to make Apollon jealous
    C. He wants to reassert his power over her
    D. He overpaid her earlier and is entitled to a free session

17. Why does the Underground Man think that sometimes $2 \times 2 = 5$ is better than $2 \times 2 = 4$?

    A. He is thinking about chaos theory
    B. He is irritated with the importance of reason in society
    C. He hates mathematics with a passion
    D. He never learned mathematics in school

18. Why did the Underground Man retire from his job in civil service?

    A. He got a better position in the military
    B. He wrote a best-selling novel
    C. He wanted to become a fulltime "lazybones"
    D. He inherited a modest sum of money

19. Why was the Underground Man's job so low-ranking?

    A. He had a bad attitude and never got promoted
    B. He quit a more prestigious job because it reminded him too much of his negative experience at school
    C. His health problems prevented him from doing any strenuous work
    D. He was not particularly talented in any area

20. Why does the Underground Man insist on going to dinner with Simonov and his friends?

    A. He wants to gain their respect
    B. He wants to poison their champagne
    C. He is hoping he will get to spend time with Olympia at the brothel
    D. He wants a free dinner because he is low on money

21. Why does the Underground Man follow the other men to the brothel, despite all of the reasons to turn back?

    A. He feels that he must encounter reality
    B. He wants to spend time with Olympia
    C. He wants to repay money he borrowed from Simonov
    D. He has already paid for the coach

22. Why does the Underground Man refuse to go to a doctor about his liver problem?

    A. He cannot afford to pay a doctor
    B. He believes it is his fate to die from liver disease
    C. He knows the problem is not very serious
    D. He resents the fact that the doctor is the only person who can help him, and refuses to go out of spite

23. Why did the Underground Man spend a lot of his time reading when he was a young man?

    A. His job required that he be familiar with literature
    B. He was bored out of his mind
    C. He needed distraction from his inner torment, and reading was the only external stimuli he could bear
    D. He wanted to learn how to improve society

24. Why does the Underground Man run into the street after Liza when she leaves his apartment?

    A. She has forgotten her handbag
    B. He wants to have the last word and insult her
    C. He wants to make sure she gets home safely
    D. He is moved by her dignity and wants to ask her forgiveness

25. Why does the Underground Man claim to address his audience in his *Notes from Underground*?

    A. He thinks they will enjoy the story more if he shows that he is interested in their opinions
    B. He needs to pretend to himself that he has a reason for organizing the notes and improving the writing style
    C. He is hoping they will give him money
    D. He wants to publicly humiliate them by refuting their arguments with perfect logic and wit

Answer Key:
1: B; 2: D; 3: B; 4: C; 5: C; 6: D; 7: A; 8: C; 9: A; 10: C;
11: C; 12: A; 13: B; 14: C; 15: B; 16: C; 17: B; 18: D; 19: B;
20: A; 21: A; 22: D; 23: C; 24: D; 25: B

SUGGESTIONS FOR FURTHER READING

COCKRELL, ROGER, ed. *The Voice of a Giant: Essays on Seven Russian Prose Classics.* Exeter, UK: University of Exeter Press, 1985.

COX, GARY. *Tyrant and Victim in Dostoevsky.* Bloomington, Indiana: Slavica Publishers, 1984.

DOSTOEVSKY, FYODOR. *Crime and Punishment.* Trans. Jessie Coulson. New York: W. W. Norton & Company, 1989.

———. *The Idiot.* Trans. Alan Myers. New York: Oxford University Press, 1998.

———. *The Brothers Karamazov.* Trans. Richard Pevear and Larissa Volokhonsky. New York: Farrar Straus & Giroux, 2002.

———. *Selected Letters of Fyodor Dostoevsky.* Ed. Joseph Frank. New Brunswick, New Jersey: Rutgers University Press, 1987.

FRANK, JOSEPH. *Dostoevsky: The Stir of Liberation, 1860-1865.* Princeton, New Jersey: Princeton University Press, 1986.

GIRARD, RENE. *Resurrection from the Underground: Fyodor Dostoevsky.* New York: Crossroad Publishing, 1997.

MILLER, ROBYN FEUER, ed. *Critical Essays on Dostoevsky.* Boston: G.K. Hall, 1986.

PEACE, RICHARD ARTHUR. *Dostoyevsky's* NOTES FROM UNDERGROUND. Bristol, UK: Bristol Classics Press, 1993.

WASIOLEK, EDWARD. *Dostoevsky: The Major Fiction.* Cambridge, Massachusetts: MIT Press, 1964.

SparkNotes Test Preparation Guides

The SparkNotes team figured it was time to cut standardized tests down to size. We've studied the tests for you, so that SparkNotes test prep guides are:

Smarter:

Packed with critical-thinking skills and test-taking strategies that will improve your score.

Better:

Fully up to date, covering all new features of the tests, with study tips on every type of question.

Faster:

Our books cover exactly what you need to know for the test. No more, no less.

SparkNotes Guide to the SAT & PSAT
SparkNotes Guide to the SAT & PSAT—Deluxe Internet Edition
SparkNotes Guide to the ACT
SparkNotes Guide to the ACT—Deluxe Internet Edition
SparkNotes Guide to the SAT II Writing
SparkNotes Guide to the SAT II U.S. History
SparkNotes Guide to the SAT II Math Ic
SparkNotes Guide to the SAT II Math IIc
SparkNotes Guide to the SAT II Biology
SparkNotes Guide to the SAT II Physics

SparkNotes Study Guides:

1984
The Adventures of Huckleberry Finn
The Adventures of Tom Sawyer
The Aeneid
All Quiet on the Western Front
And Then There Were None
Angela's Ashes
Animal Farm
Anne of Green Gables
Anthem
Antony and Cleopatra
As I Lay Dying
As You Like It
The Awakening
The Bean Trees
The Bell Jar
Beloved
Beowulf
Billy Budd
Black Boy
Bless Me, Ultima
The Bluest Eye
Brave New World
The Brothers Karamazov
The Call of the Wild
Candide
The Canterbury Tales
Catch-22
The Catcher in the Rye
The Chosen
Cold Mountain
Cold Sassy Tree
The Color Purple
The Count of Monte Cristo
Crime and Punishment
The Crucible
Cry, the Beloved Country
Cyrano de Bergerac
David Copperfield
Death of a Salesman
The Diary of a Young Girl
Doctor Faustus
A Doll's House
Don Quixote
Dr. Jekyll and Mr. Hyde
Dracula
Dune
Emma
Ethan Frome
Fahrenheit 451
Fallen Angels
A Farewell to Arms
Flowers for Algernon
The Fountainhead
Frankenstein
The Glass Menagerie
Gone With the Wind
The Good Earth
The Grapes of Wrath
Great Expectations
The Great Gatsby
Grendel
Gulliver's Travels
Hamlet
The Handmaid's Tale
Hard Times
Harry Potter and the Sorcerer's Stone
Heart of Darkness
Henry IV, Part I
Henry V
Hiroshima
The Hobbit
The House of the Seven Gables
I Know Why the Caged Bird Sings
The Iliad
Inferno
Invisible Man
Jane Eyre
Johnny Tremain
The Joy Luck Club
Julius Caesar
The Jungle
The Killer Angels
King Lear
The Last of the Mohicans
Les Misérables
A Lesson Before Dying
The Little Prince
Little Women
Lord of the Flies
The Lord of the Rings
Macbeth
Madame Bovary
A Man for All Seasons
The Mayor of Casterbridge
The Merchant of Venice
A Midsummer Night's Dream
Moby-Dick
Much Ado About Nothing
My Ántonia
Mythology
Narrative of the Life of Frederick Douglass
Native Son
The New Testament
Night
Notes from Underground
The Odyssey
The Oedipus Trilogy
Of Mice and Men
The Old Man and the Sea
The Old Testament
Oliver Twist
The Once and Future King
One Flew Over the Cuckoo's Nest
One Hundred Years of Solitude
Othello
Our Town
The Outsiders
Paradise Lost
A Passage to India
The Pearl
The Picture of Dorian Gray
Poe's Short Stories
A Portrait of the Artist as a Young Man
Pride and Prejudice
The Prince
A Raisin in the Sun
The Red Badge of Courage
The Republic
Richard III
Robinson Crusoe
Romeo and Juliet
The Scarlet Letter
A Separate Peace
Silas Marner
Sir Gawain and the Green Knight
Slaughterhouse-Five
Snow Falling on Cedars
Song of Solomon
The Sound and the Fury
Steppenwolf
The Stranger
A Streetcar Named Desire
The Sun Also Rises
A Tale of Two Cities
The Taming of the Shrew
The Tempest
Tess of the d'Urbervilles
Their Eyes Were Watching God
Things Fall Apart
The Things They Carried
To Kill a Mockingbird
To the Lighthouse
Treasure Island
Twelfth Night
Ulysses
Uncle Tom's Cabin
Walden
War and Peace
Wuthering Heights
A Yellow Raft in Blue Water